BMC

Safety on
Mountains

By purchasing this book you are contributing to the work of the BMC, including access & conservation and safety & skills.

Safety on **Mountains**
Copyright © 2010 British Mountaineering Council

Cover photograph: Walkers on Snowdon. © Rab / Ben Winston

A British Library Cataloguing in Publication Data entry exists for this book.

ISBN-13   978-0-903908-19-1

Published by
British Mountaineering Council
177–179 Burton Road, Manchester   M20 2BB

www.thebmc.co.uk

This book contains a number of illustrations provided by
Mountain Leader Training, Siabod Cottage, Capel Curig, Conwy   LL24 0ES
www.mountainleadertraining.org

Mountain Leader Training
Hyfforddi Arweinwyr Mynydda

This book contains maps reproduced with the permission of
Harvey, 12 – 16 Main Street, Doune   FK16 6BJ
www.harveymaps.co.uk

HARVEY

CONTENTS

Foreword

The British hills offer beauty, challenge and adventure, as well as the opportunity to keep fit and healthy. So it is no wonder that hill walking is such a popular activity, attracting people of all ages. Walking in the uplands requires a collection of skills, including navigation, route finding, and hazard avoidance. First published over thirty years ago, this new edition of Safety on Mountains provides guidance on these and other issues.

Where to begin

If new to hill walking, adopt a progressive approach to your days out, developing skills incrementally and building upon past experience. The apparent ease with which an experienced hill walker negotiates a route can be misleading, as only once a range of skills have been mastered can appropriate decisions be made to manage specific situations. Mountain Rescue teams routinely witness poor navigation, inadequate planning and simple slips as causes of hill walking incidents. In seeking to improve mountain safety, such findings inform the topics covered in this book.

No amount of reading or training can make hill walking completely safe, but the vast majority of hill walkers enjoy a lifetime exploring our uplands without mishap. This book will highlight the skills required to enjoy your adventures.

The rest is up to you!

BMC Participation Statement

The BMC recognises that climbing, hill walking and mountaineering are activities with a danger of personal injury or death. Participants in these activities should be aware of and accept these risks and be responsible for their own actions.

CHAPTER 1

AN INTRODUCTION TO HILL WALKING

Hill walking will take you away from the confines of the valleys and into the hills and mountains.

Where?

Britain is blessed with hundreds of hills and mountains, and even though none make 1400m in height, many ascents start at sea level, providing a great day's walking.

The Lake District, Snowdonia and the Scottish Highlands are classic mountain walking destinations, with Dartmoor, the Peak District, the Yorkshire Dales, the Cheviots and the Brecon Beacons offering adventure at lower altitudes. But some of these areas can still be pretty remote.

You need to be steady on your feet in the hills

Most areas have guidebooks of one sort or another, describing popular walking routes. But much enjoyment and satisfaction is gained from planning your own routes. In most walking areas there is plentiful accommodation, ranging from valley camping to hotels. Many will carry information specifically for walkers, such as suggested routes and weather forecasts.

So you want to go hill walking

A great summer day in the hills can be had with light clothing, comfortable footwear, some food, water and little else. However, this makes the bold assumption that the weather will be good or no mishap will occur, such as becoming lost, leading to a longer day out than expected. For these reasons, it is wise to be prepared for likely eventualities. Suitable hill walking equipment is covered in Chapter 2.

With steep cliffs, scree slopes and sharp ridges, a great attraction of hill walking is weaving a route through seemingly inhospitable terrain. Simple slips are a common cause of accidents in the hills, so movement skills are important to consider. Identifying and negotiating hazards is covered in Chapter 3.

A map and compass are essential when hill walking, but of little use if you do not know how to use them, so map reading and navigation are key skills to master. Map reading is about being able to interpret a map, essential when planning a route. Navigation is about being able to find your way around the hills with a map and compass. Poor planning and navigation are common causes of mountain incidents, so mastering these skills is important. However, don't feel you need to learn everything from scratch, as many map reading and navigation skills used in urban environments can be transferred to the uplands. Route planning, map reading and navigation are covered in Chapter 4.

Our hills and mountains present additional challenges in winter. When covered in snow and ice the land can look different, making navigation more difficult. The terrain can change quickly between ice covered rocks, soft snow and frozen ground, each requiring different styles of movement. These issues are covered in Chapter 5.

Spending a night in a tent high in the hills provides peace and solitude, and requires a good deal of self reliance. Ideas on what to take, where to camp and considerations for the environment you are camping in are covered in Chapter 6.

Take time to read information points

Developing skills with others can be fun

It's easy to get 'caught short' when hill walking, but without proper facilities, human waste needs to be managed appropriately. Instead of ignoring this topic, Chapter 7 provides clear guidance.

It is easy to take for granted the free and open access we have to our uplands, and to forget that many plants and animals are there too, some living quite marginal lives. The BMC's main area of work is in access and conservation, working with partner organisations to protect our freedoms, and informing walkers and climbers of their responsibilities. These issues are covered in Chapter 8.

Of the hundreds of thousands of people who explore the hills and mountains each year, an unlucky few can have an incident, ranging from the inconvenient to the life threatening. Chapter 9 provides basic first aid advice and the procedures to follow when dealing with a mountain incident.

The learning process

Once you know the skills you need, how do you go about gaining them? This book and the *Hill Walking Essentials* DVD will give you grounding in the core skills, but are no substitute for going out and developing your skills in the hills and mountains.

Whether you choose to begin your adventures alone, with another novice, or under the watchful eye of someone more experienced, what is most important is to adopt a progressive approach, building upon past experience as you learn. Different approaches suit different people and some useful contact details are available in Chapter 10. You could join one of over 300 BMC affiliated clubs running meets throughout the country; many clubs own huts, providing a great base for your trips.

Whichever learning path you choose, remember that acquiring technical skills is not the same as developing the judgement on when and where to use them. For example, walking in a straight line on a compass bearing can enable efficient navigation in poor visibility, but if the terrain is extremely boggy, adopting only this technique may result in getting extremely wet! More seriously, if there are small cliffs in the area then walking in a straight line could quickly lead into hazardous terrain.

In essence, judgement skills and technical proficiency work hand in hand and should be developed in tandem.

CHAPTER 2

CLOTHING AND EQUIPMENT

A great appeal of the British hills is that a day out can be had with minimal kit. There is not much gear that is vital, but it's important to have appropriate equipment for the activity and prevailing weather.

CLOTHING

The Three Basics

When out in the hills you will need, as a minimum:

1. Boots to keep you upright

2. Insulating layers to keep you warm

3. Waterproofs to keep you dry

Equip yourself with these three basics and even if the weather turns bad, you should be set for a great day out. On hot days a sun hat may be more useful than lots of thermals, but you should always ensure you have sufficient kit to keep you warm and dry in case you're out for longer than planned.

1. Boots to keep you upright

Twisting or even breaking an ankle is not uncommon when hill walking, and of all the summer hill walking incidents attended by Mountain Rescue Teams, about a third are the result of a slip, trip or tumble. It is not possible to conclude that inadequate footwear was a cause in these cases, but it does demonstrate the importance of choosing boots that are comfortable and provide adequate support and grip.

Boots are commonly described in relation to the seasons or activity. Their construction reflects the use they are designed for, and no boots are perfectly suited for all seasons and terrain. A lightweight summer boot would be completely inappropriate in winter, for example, just as wearing winter mountaineering boots on a hot sunny day can result in overheated and blistered feet.

Boot design

Boot construction varies greatly and affects how 'soft' or 'firm' a boot feels. Summer boots tend to flex more than winter boots, which require a stiff sole to gain purchase on snow and ice. When walking on bare rock a soft sole moulds to the uneven surface better than a firm sole.

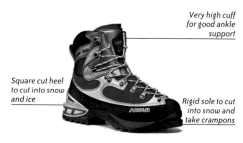

Very high cuff for good ankle support

Square cut heel to cut into snow and ice

Rigid sole to cut into snow and take crampons

Winter boot

High cuff for good ankle support

Leather upper for water repellency

Stiff sole for support

Summer and autumn boot

Heel cup provides ankle support

Breathable suede and fabric upper

Flexible sole for comfort

Summer shoe

For this reason summer boots can feel more comfortable. However, a boot with a more rigid sole can grip small edges more effectively. Such differences demonstrate why a softer boot is great for trail walking and a firmer boot better suited to scrambling.

Ankle support is provided by having high cuffs, a firm sole and heel cups. Boots with low cuffs and no cupping heel will give less support.

Insoles: The insole, also known as the footbed, is likely to be removable. A good insole will give some cushioning. If you want improved cushioning you could fit a shock absorbing insole.

Midsoles: The midsole usually consists of two parts. A plastic or nylon layer designed to give graduated stiffness appropriate to the type of boot and a further shock absorbing layer.

A useful way to gauge how much support a boot will give is by twisting it. Holding the heel in one hand and the toe box in the other see how easy the boot will twist. The easier it twists the more flexible the midsole, and so the less support the boot will provide on steep uneven terrain or steep grassy slopes. Conversely, if most of your walking is along well defined paths with gentle inclines, a softer boot may suit you better.

Outsole: A lot of design work goes into the sole, to provide the right combination of grip and durability. As already mentioned a large proportion of hill walking accidents are due to a simple slip, so the importance of having an effective sole cannot be overstated. A boot's effectiveness will be reduced as the sole wears, so resole early and don't wait until the tread is gone.

Choosing a boot

When it comes to deciding what to buy, there is a lot of choice out there! But the number and variety of boots on the market means that you should be able to find the right pair for your needs.

Approach, trail walking and one season shoes or boots

These are great on level terrain such as lowland valley tracks, or a stroll around a lowland lake. They're unlikely to keep your feet dry, even in gentle rain, and provide either limited or no ankle support. They are therefore not suitable when the ground becomes rough and uneven. They should not be confused with specialist fell running and orienteering shoes, which are even lighter.

Hill walking, trekking and two season boots

These boots will have a cuff providing some ankle support, a more aggressive tread pattern on their sole and should have some waterproof qualities. If made entirely of leather then waxes can be applied to maintain their water repellency. If the upper is a leather and fabric mix, then having an internal membrane is the best way to ensure your feet will remain dry in wet weather. Membranes may begin to fail before the rest of the boot has worn out.

Choose the right boots for the activity

Mountaineering and three to four season boots
A high ankle cuff and stiff midsole characterises these boots. Mountaineering boots designed for ice climbing or kicking steps on hard frozen snow will have a midsole that makes the boot very rigid, and so suitable for attaching crampons. Compared to a summer boot, mountaineering boots may also have insulating layers to provide warmth.

These boots may not be very comfortable if walking long distances on firm level terrain such as valley tracks or tarmac, but will provide excellent support on steep and uneven terrain.

Boots can take a hammering!

What else to consider
Some boots can be used for summer and winter walking. But whatever you choose, make sure the boot is appropriate for the most demanding conditions you plan to walk in. If you are very heavy with large feet, or very light with small feet you could also consider choosing a more or less substantial boot as appropriate.

Try the boots on with your own appropriate walking socks. Specialist walking socks have design features that affect the fit of your boot, so bear this in mind when selecting your boot size. A good fit will give you room around the toes and hold the heel to prevent it lifting too much.

Many shops will let you take the boots home for a few days' indoor trial and then let you return them if they're not quite right. Walking up and down a flight of stairs can help you decide if your foot is held firmly in the boot.

Your first long walk in a new pair of boots will help break them in. The stiffer and heavier they are, the more breaking in will be required. Be aware of any rub points, and if you notice any, stop and apply tape or a plaster which should prevent blisters developing.

Check the manufacturer's instructions for advice on care. At the end of the day your boots will be damp and should be allowed to dry slowly – not next to an open fire or on a radiator.

Socks

Good socks regulate your foot temperature and help to prevent blisters by providing a snug fit. As with your clothing, socks need to wick moisture away from your skin, as overheated feet will be uncomfortable and prone to developing blisters. When looking for a good fit, consider socks with elasticated ribbing, to prevent bunching, and gender specific designs.

Choose socks that are padded in the heel, ball and toes where the most pressure is applied. Some people like to wear two pairs of socks consisting of a snug thin inner one and a thicker outer one. This system can reduce friction on your feet, as the sock layers will move against each other instead of your feet moving against the sock.

Finally, a boot needs to be used properly. This is where movement skills come in, which are covered in the next chapter.

A layered clothing system is the most flexible

2. Insulating layers to keep you warm

Just as we use layers of clothing in our everyday lives to regulate body temperature, the same is true when exploring the hills. There are a number of major differences however between what is required of clothing in the urban environment, and that suitable for the uplands.

The range of temperatures experienced in one day will often be greater in the hills than in cities. Clothing to deal with such variation is therefore required. You will need to wear or carry all your clothing, and with the weight of your rucksack an important consideration, choosing items that fulfil a range of functions is a good idea. Waterproofs double up as windproofs for example.

Instead of thinking what specific clothing to take, consider the principles, as you may find you already own clothing that fits the bill very well. Common sense dictates that you need light comfortable clothing while you walk, something warm for when it gets colder and something waterproof in case the heavens open.

Finally, emergencies do occur, often resulting in walkers staying put for extended periods of time. Being able to keep warm and dry in such situations is very important.

It's all about the layers

As already mentioned, it is much better to wear several relatively thin layers rather than one very thick one. This is because the layers trap air which is a good insulator, and you can regulate your temperature more effectively by adding or removing layers.

Materials which do not absorb moisture are better because wet clothes will make you feel cold. Wool has always been recognised as a good material for hill walkers and it is having a comeback with the

Fleece jackets are good thermal layers

advent of modern wool based fabrics. Synthetic materials such as fleece are also used for outdoor clothing. Cotton is not good and jeans are particularly cold when wet.

Most people already have some suitable insulating layers before they start hill walking, such as a thin wicking baselayer and light woollen midlayer. The baselayer should wick moisture away from your body, and so keep your skin dry and prevent excessive chilling every time you stop. As well as providing insulation, a thin midlayer also allows moisture to wick.

Fleece jackets are excellent as a third insulating layer. You can pay a lot of money for a high end fleece or buy one relatively cheaply. The quality and fit will vary, but both should work adequately well. As fleeces wear out they become a lot thinner, losing much of their insulating properties.

All these layers should be relatively snug on your body. If too tight they will obviously be uncomfortable, but if loose and baggy then instead of trapping warm air you're likely to have cold drafts instead!

Leg muscles produce a lot of heat when we walk and thermal leg wear is likely only to be necessary in cold conditions.

Even though cotton is seen as inappropriate in our predominately wet climate because it holds water, a loose long sleeved cotton shirt can work well on hot sunny days, protecting the body from sunburn and overheating.

Gloves

These need not be over specialised. A simple pair of woollen or fleece gloves or mittens will be fine. As with socks, a spare pair weighs very little but at times can be vital. Gloves that are better at retaining warmth when wet are a real advantage, such as thick woollen ones or those with a windproof outer.

Even expensive waterproof gloves are unlikely to keep your hands dry in extreme conditions. Only in winter should you be really concerned about your hands getting so cold that they become prone to frostnip or even frostbite. In such cold environments mittens are often preferable, as they are warmer than gloves.

Head gear

On cold days, a hat or balaclava and scarf or neck gaiter will reduce the heat lost through the head and neck. Fleece is probably the most popular material as it is light and flexible. It can also be wrung dry if it gets very wet. A fleece ear band can also be very welcome in winter to keep those extremities toasty warm!

Wearing a sunhat and neckerchief is a good idea on hot sunny days, as they will protect the head and neck from sunburn and overheating. If the body absorbs more heat than it can dissipate then heatstroke (also known as hyperthermia or sunstroke) could ensue, which is a serious medical condition. When it's hot and sunny, drinking plenty of liquid is very important, and two litres of water could easily be required. But wearing appropriate clothing will also help keep the body cool.

Keep your head warm and you will be warm!

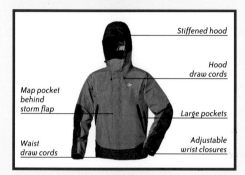

Stiffened hood

Hood draw cords

Map pocket behind storm flap

Large pockets

Waist draw cords

Adjustable wrist closures

Hill walking jacket

3. Waterproofs to keep you dry

It may be sunny as you start your day, but it could rain later. This is not to imply that there is no way of knowing what the weather will do, as there are excellent web and telephone based mountain weather forecasts available. However, a forecast is just that, a prediction of what should happen. Even in stable high pressure weather systems, violent afternoon showers are commonplace, especially in the mountains.

Nowadays, just about all waterproofs are made from breathable fabrics, allowing body moisture to escape, whilst keeping the rain out. Non breathable fabrics do not let perspiration escape, so you can get increasingly damp as the day wears on.

Waterproof material is often made up of three bonded layers, with the waterproof membrane sandwiched in the middle. As well as being less well cut, cheaper waterproofs may wear out more quickly, as the outer layer will be thin and not very tough. However, a thinner outer layer will make the waterproofs lighter and more breathable, and for gentle walking with a small rucksack may work best. Conversely, if you commonly carry quite a lot or go on multi day trips, then tougher waterproofs could be worth the investment.

Jackets

Waterproof jackets vary a lot in price, but you should not conclude that expensive jackets are more water-proof than cheaper versions. More complicated designs providing a better fit, or more pockets and underarm vents take longer to make and cost more than a cheaper model, but both could be made from the same materials and be equally waterproof.

Some features are often worth the cost, however. A stiffened hood helps maintain good visibility, as the alternative is one that slaps you in the face with every gust of wind!

Some general jacket features to consider include:

- Big enough to get warm layers underneath, but not so big that it flaps around.

- An easily accessible pocket that can accommodate a map.

- Large pockets for carrying hats, gloves, and so on.

- Waist and hood drawcords.

- Adjustable wrist closures.

- Stiffened hood.

Trousers

Waterprooof trousers are more likely to get ripped than jackets, so consider the wear resistance of the material they are made from. More expensive trousers with more seams should be better cut, making them more comfortable. Trousers can have the annoying habit of sliding down, creating a cold spot in your lower back. Some come with elastic braces to keep them up.

You'll need to be able to put your trousers on and remove them whilst wearing your boots, so make sure there are zips down the side. Full length zips are essential if you intend to wear crampons, but zips reaching only the knees work fine for summer hill walking.

Gaiters

Gaiters can be invaluable on boggy ground and rainy days. They also prove useful when walking through heather, preventing twigs and other vegetation from entering your boots. On dry days or if walking on well defined paths, then they may seem like overkill. As with all clothing layers, gaiters will provide a barrier to moisture leaving the body, so ones made from breathable fabrics can be more comfortable. When walking in winter, gaiters are pretty much indispensible. It does not take much snow in your boots before your feet become cold and wet.

If worn in conjunction with waterproof trousers, wear the gaiters underneath. With the gaiters on the outside and trousers tucked in, water will be 'conveniently' channelled into your boots!

Under-boot fixings prevent gaiters from riding up above your boot cuffs. The fixings should be durable, but most importantly you should be able to replace them, as you can pretty much guarantee that they will wear out before the gaiter. Zips on gaiters will also fail long before the material, and many models now use Velcro instead. This is both quicker and easier to use than a zip.

Gaiters covering the whole of the boot are available, but are not necessary when hill walking. Walking on rocky paths can quickly degrade their rubber rands, which are then quite expensive to replace. Such full boot protection and insulation is more appropriate for extreme environments such as the Himalaya.

EQUIPMENT

Rucksacks

A rucksack is the most convenient way to carry your equipment, and should be neither too big nor too small. When full, it should be comfortable to wear. There are many different sizes to choose from, each appropriate for different activities. When moorland walking, a 30 litre rucksack is probably adequate; if heading into the mountains, a 45 litre rucksack would be better; and if camping overnight, a bigger rucksack will be required.

For a rucksack to be comfortable when full of equipment, it needs to fit the wearer's back and distribute the load evenly. All walkers should consider their own back anatomy in relation to the rucksack they choose. The shoulder-waist-hip ratios are different between men and women, and so some rucksacks are specially designed for women.

As back length is critical when it comes to comfort, some rucksacks have adjustable back systems to ensure a correct fit for each individual. Such rucksacks will also be heavier and more expensive than a simpler design of the same volume.

In relation to fit, when wearing a full rucksack, here are some things to consider:

- The rucksack should be close to the wearer's back, allowing for an upright posture to be maintained. The further away from the back the rucksack sits, the more the walker has to bend forward when walking, to counterbalance the weight of the rucksack. Some rucksacks have removable foam backs with malleable metal guides that can be bent to conform to the wearer's back, bringing the rucksack closer in.

Small day walk rucksack

- With the rucksack resting on the shoulders and snug on the back, the hip belt should sit on the hips when buckled up. It should be possible to adjust shoulder straps and hip belt to distribute the load between the hips and shoulders. Taller people may need to choose a rucksack with a longer back.

- People with wide necks or very broad shoulders should avoid rucksacks where the shoulder straps dig into the back of the neck. They may find a wider rucksack more comfortable.

- When wearing a rucksack, it should be possible to tilt the head backwards. If the rucksack sits very high on the back then the neck cannot move freely. Also, with the load high, the rucksack will feel unwieldy, increasing the chance of losing balance and falling over.

With regard to general rucksack design:

- A slim profile with no side pockets is less likely to get caught on obstructions such as rocks, fence posts, or bushes. Placing heavy items such as bottles and flasks in side pockets can make the rucksack feel lop sided.

- Compression straps along the side of the rucksack allow a slim profile to be maintained, and can be used to secure walking poles when not in use.

- Inside and outside lid pockets are very useful. The former for valuables and the latter for gloves, hats and snacks.

- If the seams are held together with only one row of stitching, then do not be surprised if the sack falls apart more quickly than expected.

Finally, consider how to pack your rucksack. Regularly used items should be easily accessible in the lid pocket or top of the rucksack. Heavy items, such as water bottles or thermos flasks, should be packed close to the back in the middle portion of the rucksack. Light items, such as fleece clothing, can be packed further away from the back of the rucksack. Distributing weight in this way will result in better stability when walking.

Packing kit in a selection of drybags is the best way to prevent it getting wet. Hats and gloves in one bag; spare clothing in another, for example. On rainy days especially, not having to expose all your kit to the elements at one time makes life much easier. Small transparent drybags are also available for mobile phones and GPS devices. Heavy duty carrier bags are a cheaper alternative to drybags.

Map and compass

Navigation is covered in Chapter 4, but when it comes to your map and compass, make sure you know how to use them and that they are always close to hand. Some jackets have convenient map pockets located behind the storm flap, and a compass can be worn around the neck.

If your map and compass skills are not up to it, then learn how to navigate in the valleys and on the low hills, before heading up higher. You could join a club and learn from more experienced walkers, read *Navigation in the Mountains* or watch the *Hill Walking Essentials* DVD. Both publications are packed with useful information on navigation and route finding. As already mentioned, Mountain Rescue Teams regularly attend incidents where walkers have become lost.

GPS handsets

The Global Positioning System (GPS) is a collection of 24 earth orbiting satellites. Using the signals they send, a small GPS handset can pinpoint position to within 15m on average, a great benefit when hill walking.

Check your location throughout the day

There is a big difference however between knowing where you are, and being able to plan and follow an appropriate route. Owning a GPS handset should therefore not be seen as a substitute for map reading and navigational skills. Instead, they should be seen as a useful supplementary navigational tool.

GPS handsets and mapping software are covered in the Chapter 4.

Trekking poles

Trekking poles are increasingly popular, and are best used as a pair. Poor technique can negate any positive benefits, and there are pros and cons to using them.

A pair of poles provides more support than just one

Pros

- After a long day out in the hills, aching knees on the descent is very common. Poles can transfer some of the impact of walking from the lower legs and knees to the arms and shoulders.

- Poles also help with stability, particularly useful when carrying a heavy sack, walking on uneven ground or in winter when patches of ice can occur unexpectedly.

- Walking with poles can be quite rhythmic, helping maintain a steady pace.

Cons

- The wrist, elbow and shoulder joints are not designed to prop up your body – we're bipedal after all! If you're not careful, protecting your knees can simply mean aggravating other joints. Therefore, always try to use the muscles, as opposed to pushing the joints to their extremes. This is especially important when putting a lot of force through the pole. Keep your hand in a neutral position whenever possible, as this uses the muscles. Having it continually bent upwards puts more of the load on the wrist joint.

- If you are very tired and do not need the poles for stability, it may be best to pack them away if there is the chance of tripping yourself up on one!

- Using poles prevents your hands from being free for other things. Don't fall into the trap of not eating, drinking or checking your map simply because you cannot be bothered to take your poles off. And when ascending a short frozen slope with poles, then you should really get your ice axe out.

Sunscreen

A cooling mountain breeze on a hot sunny day can easily lead to the assumption that there is little chance of getting sunburn. This is obviously far from true! If the sun is out, applying sunscreen and lip-salve in advance and then regularly throughout the day is the way to go.

Snow and water reflect much more UV light than bare earth, and on a clear winter's day sunscreen should be applied to the face, and the undersides of your chin and ears.

Sunglasses and goggles

It goes without saying that sunglasses can make life more comfortable on a sunny summer's day. In winter, not wearing some eye protection can make it very hard to move around or even lead to snow blindness. This is a reversible condition caused by unprotected eyes being exposed to UV light reflected from the snow, and is akin to parts of the eyes being sunburnt. Goggles are essential bits of winter kit, and covered in Chapter 5.

Insect repellent

In Scotland especially, midges can be the bane of the summer hill walker, but repellents containing DEET work well to stop them biting. Some people do not like using DEET based repellents, preferring those containing natural ingredients such as Citronella, but these are not as effective as DEET based products. If camping in the summer, consider taking a mesh head net for extra protection.

Food and drink

As crucial as taking suitable equipment is having sufficient food and drink. The amount required will vary depending on weather conditions, distance and terrain walked. On a warm summer's day you will suffer if you skimp on the drink, and in winter you need a good quantity of food and drink to keep warm. A hot drink is likely to be very welcome, with a metal thermos flask being more robust than a glass one.

A good breakfast will set you up for a day's walk, and while out, consuming little and often is the best way to keep hydrated and maintain your energy. It is sensible to have some emergency food, like high energy bars, tucked away 'just in case'.

You do not need to take any 'specialist' food; sandwiches, snacks and some fruit will work fine. But just as in everyday life, eating lots of sugary food is not a good idea when hill walking as your energy levels could swing dramatically.

Quick snacks help maintain energy

When it comes to drinks, water will do the job perfectly well, but be careful if taking water from streams. In theory, running water without a farm or habitation up stream should be fine, but in recent years there have been increasing reports of pathogens such as giardia being found in some streams. This is probably due to poor human waste management when wild camping.

Having a medical condition such as diabetes or any restrictive dietary requirements which can affect the body's energy levels should not be seen as a barrier to enjoying our hills and mountains.

Dealing with emergencies

If things don't go according to plan it's important to stay calm. Getting lost can be quite distressing, for example, but if no one is in any danger then there is no need to panic. Even if someone has been injured, what's most important is to ensure that the situation does not escalate into something yet more serious. Always give yourself time to think, instead of rushing headlong into a hastily made plan of action. Chapter 9 provides practical information on First Aid and managing a mountain incident, but here are suggestions for some simple yet effective emergency equipment to take.

First Aid Kit

When dealing with an injured hill walker, help will not immediately be close at hand. Therefore, taking a first aid kit and seeking out some basic first aid training is a very good idea. Some first aid courses are specifically designed for remote environments and provide guidance on incident management and dealing with common situations.

Group shelter

Getting lost in poor visibility or dealing with even a minor injury can escalate into something more serious for the whole party if people get cold. Spare clothing should be carried for this reason, but a group shelter is the most effective way to keep warm.

Made from light ripstop nylon, a group shelter is shaped like a very large upside down bowl. Stood in a circle facing each other, the group pull it over their heads and down their backs, before tucking it under their legs and sitting down. The warmer temperature inside the shelter is created by shared body warmth and lack of wind.

Possessing basic first aid skills can be very useful

Group shelters also provide time for a drink and check of the map

If someone gets hurt you may need outside help

Don't forget it gets dark at night!

As well as being great in emergency situations, group shelters are perfect for quick breaks in poor weather if only to look at the map and collect your thoughts. Once insulated from the outside, calm is restored, and spirits are raised.

Bivi bag

Made from tough orange polythene, a bivi bag provides individual shelter in case of emergency. Effective and inexpensive, they can be used in conjunction with a group shelter. An injured walker who is placed inside a bivi bag and insulated from the ground, will be best positioned in the centre of the whole group. The more expensive Blizzard Survival Bag provides greater insulating properties than a standard polythene bivi bag.

Torch

It is not uncommon for mountain rescue teams to assist able bodied walkers off the hills who have simply got caught out after dark. Whether underestimating how long a walk will take, or getting lost and staying out for longer than planned, heading back home in the dark need not be a reason to panic if everyone has a torch. A headtorch is best, and many inexpensive models are widely available. Always take a torch and make sure you also have some spare batteries.

In winter, when the days are much shorter and the terrain can be more challenging, it would be extremely foolhardy not to pack a torch.

Mobile phone

Mobile phones can be a godsend when needing to contact the emergency services, but should not be thought of as a 'safety net', tempting walkers to objectives outside of their experience and ability.

When used in an emergency, call 999, ask for the Police and then Mountain Rescue. Keep your phone on and try to give accurate details on where you are. It is well worth remembering that if you have no signal then walking 10 minutes uphill may be a lot more effective than 10 minutes downhill. If you are lost then the team will ask you to describe your location and will often be able to talk you down. When the Mountain Rescue Team is nearby you will be asked to make lots of noise. A whistle is handy for this, as are a good pair of lungs!

Winter evening light

Winter equipment

As a general rule, winter boots and clothing should be more substantial than those used in summer. This does not mean that you need to go out and buy a new wardrobe, but that extra insulating layers, thicker (and spare) gloves, a warm hat, tough waterproofs and appropriate boots are all required.

Before heading out it is worth noting that winter conditions can occur in the British hills throughout much of the year. Snow or ice on the ground and blizzard conditions are possible in early spring and late autumn, and walkers equipped only for a summer hike would be under equipped to deal with such conditions. When accidents occur, the whole party is at risk of developing hypothermia. To counter this, a group shelter and spare warm clothing are key components of a winter kit list.

The most important extra equipment required is an ice axe and a pair of crampons. If you do not know how to use these then you would be best learning from someone more experienced. Download the *BMC Crampons and Ice Axes booklet* from our website for technical information. Practical guidance is available from the BMC *Winter Essentials* DVD and the *Winter Skills* book published by Mountain Leader Training. Chapter 5 of this book also considers a range of issues when out winter walking.

Finally, as with summer hill walking making good judgements is key in winter. The snow pack changes over time, with relatively stable slopes sometimes becoming highly avalanche prone in a matter of hours. With the ground covered in snow, navigation is much more challenging, and route finding more demanding. By adopting a progressive approach and being honest as to your current ability, a competent summer hill walker will be able to develop their winter mountaineering skills.

CHAPTER 3

HAZARDS

Planning and then following a route through the hills, and successfully managing the hazards along the way, is a sign of good judgement. But just as a young child has to learn about hazards in their world, novice hill walkers will encounter challenges which are new to them.

Identifying hazards

Dealing with hazards is part of everyday life, so consider the strategies you commonly use. Imagine stepping into the road only to see a car speeding towards you. In an instant, you would identify the hazard, assess the risk, and then act appropriately. Or in other words – get out of the way! When it comes to hazards in the hills, follow the same process of identify, assess and act.

Listen to your instincts, and stop if something doesn't feel 'quite right'. If you still feel unsure after assessing the situation then choose a different route. Even if that means a long detour or not bagging your summit, changing your plans due to unforeseen circumstances is a sign of good judgement. Carrying blindly on with the hope that 'things will work themselves out' is not!

It is important to realise that you cannot avoid hazards. Before setting out ask yourself what hazards are presented by the terrain, group members and the weather. Reassess hazards throughout the day.

TERRAIN

Look at the map before leaving and see where your route will take you. Are there streams or rivers to cross? If so, is there a bridge? Can a navigational error lead you into serious terrain, such as steep slopes where the ground might be loose? As the saying goes, 'To be forewarned is to be forearmed.' If you know what to expect you will be much better placed to deal with it.

Plans often have to be changed along the way. Previous heavy rain could result in boggy ground requiring a detour, for example. Being able to make dynamic risk assessments and flexibility in your planning are both important skills to develop.

Movement skills

A simple slip is one of the most common causes of injury to hill walkers, and the more uneven or steeper the ground, the greater the potential for a slip.

Those new to hill walking may find the uneven and variable terrain challenging at first. Wearing a pair of good boots is very important, but using them effectively is what will get you around the hills.

Good foot placements will help you position your centre of balance over your feet as you walk. You can consider any object's centre of balance as the point where it is in balance. A pencil, for example, can be balanced at its midpoint, and a plate at its centre.

Don't slip at the wrong moment!

As we have left / right symmetry, and as our upper and lower bodies each weigh about the same, our centre of balance is positioned a little way below the middle of an imaginary line running from the navel to the spine. A rucksack will 'pull' the centre of balance further back (and a little higher), and to compensate for this it is necessary to lean slightly forward when wearing one.

When walking on flat surfaces, such as a pavement, it is pretty straightforward to maintain your balance. When out in the hills, walking on uneven terrain, taking small steps will make it easier to keep your centre of balance over your feet.

Making a stable platform with each step, using as much of the sole as possible is also important, as with only part of the sole in contact you will be less stable. It is easier to make such a platform on grassy and muddy slopes with stiffer boots than with trail shoes and soft boots.

Walking up, down and across

Steep ground is always easier to ascend in control than it is to traverse or descend. You should always know how you are going to get back down before you start to climb. If the descent is steep, then it may be more time consuming and difficult than expected.

The ground ahead is close at hand when ascending, and with short steps, foot placements are easy to spot. On descents, in contrast, you have to extend downwards with each step, making placements more difficult to settle on. Trekking poles can help greatly in these situations.

Avoid leaning back in descent, as this will take weight off your feet increasing the chance of you slipping backwards. A more stable descending position can be gained by flexing your ankle, knee and hip joints and so lowering your centre of balance and placing it over your feet. Practice in secure places on short slopes.

The tendency when traversing is to creep down the slope. In some situations this may not be a problem, but traversing a steep slope for a long time can be very tiring. Routes taking in such terrain can feel like a slog!

Lowering the body's centre of balance on descent

Grass slopes

When involved in technical and demanding hill walking, you will be focused on the challenges at hand, but on easier ground it is tempting to relax and lose concentration. Steep grass slopes can be extremely hazardous, not only in wet conditions, but also when the grass is long and dry.

Walkers should be aware that it is not the ground underfoot that defines the seriousness of a situation, but the consequences of a fall. An unbroken steep grassy slope may be more serious than a steeper, but short rocky slope.

Scree

Scree, composed of loose surface rocks, is commonly encountered in the mountains, and due to its unstable nature is often tiring to ascend. In wet conditions, scree can be extremely unpleasant to cross, being both unstable and slippery, and great care should be taken. To conserve energy, concentrate on foot placements to maximise the security that can be found.

Care should be taken in descent and 'scree running' should be avoided, as it accelerates erosion and is environmentally damaging. Scree running is sliding down with the flow of the scree instead of taking small footsteps, thus minimising the movement of the scree.

Steep and loose ground must be taken with care

Creating a flat platform on a grassy slope

Scrambling in some exhilarating scenery

Rocks

Many classic walking routes may have one or more short rocky steps, sections where care and attention is required. A scramble could be thought of as a route with several steep rocky steps. The North Ridge of Tryfan in North Wales is one well known scramble. Though not technically demanding, the consequences of a fall in the wrong place could be very serious.

Confidence in your movement skills is vital when the going gets more demanding; be aware that rock steps can be more challenging in descent than ascent. Therefore, if a bit more adventure is what makes you tick, adopt a progressive approach to your days out, building on past experiences as you develop new skills.

Loose rock tumbling down the hillside is also a hazard. If walking where you think there might be loose rock above, consider if any people or animals could dislodge rocks onto you.

Hidden hazards

A concave slope is shaped like the inside of a bowl, shallow at the bottom and steep at the top. This allows its whole length to be viewed, from above or below, and a route planned. A convex slope is shaped like a dome, shallow at the top and steeply sided. This means that the view of what lies ahead is often obscured.

Ascending a convex slope can be frustrating. Just as you think you're near the summit, more of the hill comes into view. In descent, a convex slope may hide real dangers such as a line of cliffs, a steep grass slope or a snow patch.

The contours describing a concave slope will be close together near the top and then widen as the slope becomes shallow. The opposite is the case for a convex slope, with the contours wide apart near the top and then closer together as the slope steepens. Noticing such patterns on a map will help with route planning, and map symbols will show if any hazards lie en route. The Navigation chapter has more information on these topics.

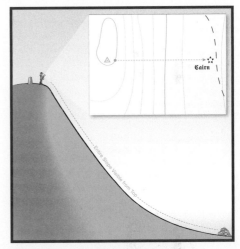

Concave Slope – cairn and path visible from above

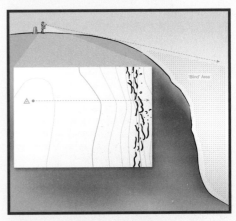

Convex Slope – cliff hazard not visible from above

Water hazards

It is fair to say that high rainfall is a characteristic of our hills and mountains. Consequently, the water levels of streams, rivers, bogs and lakes can vary greatly throughout the year. Prolonged heavy rainfall can lead to flash flooding, with paths being transformed into streams.

Unless intending to swim in a mountain lake, no one plans to get wet when out walking. Considering that people do drown in upland rivers and lakes, avoiding water hazards is the best policy.

Marshes and bogs

Being covered in vegetation, marshy land is not always spotted until your feet feel wet and you experience that sinking feeling! Marshy ground can usually be indentified by a change in vegetation from shorter grasses to taller reeds. Bogs are usually covered in mosses such as sphagnum which are often bright green. Water obviously collects in hollows so the shape of the land will also provide some clues. You would be very unlucky to drown in a marsh or bog, but you can get very wet and smelly, so it is best to make a detour wherever possible. If you do cross a marsh or bog move tentatively, weight your feet slowly with every step.

Lakes

Large expanses of open water are usually pretty obvious, but smaller tarns, lochans and llyns can be overlooked. Even though not very wide, they can be quite deep and often do not have shallow sides. When frozen over in winter, they may be tempting to cross, but it is very difficult to gauge the strength of the ice, and falling in would be extremely serious. In poor visibility, the fringes of a lake can be mistaken for marshy ground as they both have similar vegetation.

Rivers and streams

Falling in a river or stream will mean getting wet at best, so a bridge is always the preferred way to cross, even if that means a long walk. Hill walkers have drowned in even benign looking mountain streams so never underestimate the threat posed by moving water. If you decide to make a crossing then ensure you make full consideration of the consequences of a slip.

Many crossings are made by hopping across on boulders, just as you might cross a boulder field, which poses the risk of falling over and banging your head. The extra threat posed by water is that of being both concussed and submerged.

If a slip means getting wet, standing up and continuing to the other side, then the risks are still serious, as wet clothing will make you cold. If a slip means being washed away, then the risks are very high, and you should question your reasons for crossing.

Even short periods of heavy rain can cause rivers to rise rapidly, often making them impassable, and crossing a river or stream which is in flood should not be attempted. If heavy rain is forecast then think whether your planned route will require you to cross any rivers or streams late in the day by which time this may not be possible.

Two DVDs produced by the Mountaineering Council of Scotland, and the Mountain Leader Training's *Hill Walking* book, provide much detail on various crossing techniques, which are not discussed here. Instead, some of the obvious and less obvious hazards are listed.

Water course hazards

Be aware that:

- The strength of the water flow is easily under-estimated, and fast water does not have to be very deep to knock you off your feet.

- Water conducts heat away from the body 20 to 30 times more quickly than air. Once clothes are wet, there is a real risk of developing hypothermia.

- River and stream beds are both slippery and uneven. Considering that your view is also obscured, it can be difficult to secure good foot placements.

- There may be downstream obstacles such as trees, boulders and waterfalls. Some can be hidden under the surface, making them hard to spot.

Assessing a crossing point

If you do need to get wet consider a crossing point where the water is shallow, narrow and slow. It goes without saying that these three attributes will make for a safer crossing point than one which is deep, wide and fast.

Keep your boots and socks on. Not only will you then be more stable, your feet and ankles are also protected. Socks can always be wrung out when wet. Rucksack straps should be loosened so that rucksacks can be taken off in an emergency.

Unlike other hill walking skills, dealing with water hazards is not one to practise. In most cases, crossing a serious river or stream would be an emergency action rather than part of a planned day. The sensible action is to avoid crossings altogether, as they should only be considered as a last resort.

Only cross streams if you have to

Look out for others on rocky steps

GROUP MEMBERS

If there is a mismatch between group members in their ability and fitness, then consideration needs to be given to how the day can meet everyone's aspirations. Added into this mix are people who may be over ambitious in what they and others can achieve. Needless to say, managing group dynamics is not always easy, even if only two people are involved! Make an honest appraisal of what is realistic for the whole group.

Mountain Rescue Teams regularly attend people who made poor decisions. Some decisions result in serious situations, such as walkers stranded on steep terrain way beyond their ability, and others are more benign, such as getting caught out on a warm summer night without a torch.

The common factor is that people made the decisions leading to the incidents occurring, and it is a sobering thought to realise that you and your group members can present a hazard through your actions and inactions.

In mixed ability groups, more experienced walkers can find themselves making decisions on behalf of other group members, such as choosing which route to take or navigating in poor visibility. In these situations it is important to distinguish between whether or not someone is leading a group, or simply happy to provide a view when key decisions need to be taken.

The dynamics within the whole group are likely to be different if people think they are being led or simply advised, with the former more likely to result in less experienced people taking a back seat. It can also be unfair on an experienced walker who is more than happy to share their knowledge, but does not wish to feel they are also responsible for less experienced group members.

Learning from experienced hill walkers is undoubtedly effective and rewarding for all involved. But this does not mean that those with less experience are not also able to make key decisions about their own safety and participation.

Clouds in the mountains

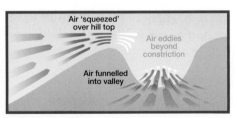
Air channelled by the hills

WEATHER

Talking about the weather is a national pastime. Our variable and predominantly wet weather is the result of the British Isles being located at the boundary between two very different air masses, providing us all with endless opportunities to discuss it. Before setting out always get a weather forecast and, if possible, a mountain specific one as there are major differences between urban and upland weather. Use the information from the forecast as a vital part of your planning. More weather information is available in *Hill Walking*, published by Mountain Leader Training.

General weather forecasts focus on temperature and precipitation. Unless it is likely to be very blowy, wind speeds are not always mentioned, but strong winds can be a real problem when walking in the hills. General forecasts are for sea level, and you can pretty much guarantee that it will be colder, wetter and windier the higher you climb. It is important to be aware that the weather can be more extreme in the hills than in the cities.

Not only should hill walkers develop their understanding of the typical British weather systems, they should also learn how to interpret a sea level forecast for the mountain environment. In addition to this is the crucial connection between a forecast and how the weather will feel, how this will impact upon your plans, and what alternative routes might need to be taken. Finally, as forecasts are just a prediction, the weather you experience could be more or less severe than that forecast.

Wind

The part of the Earth's atmosphere where weather systems occur is called the troposphere. On average it is 17km high, meaning that a large obstruction, such as a mountain, will reduce the distance between the ground and the top of the troposphere. Just as a narrowing in a river makes the water flow faster, so a narrowing in the troposphere will make the air move faster. This means that wind speeds increase the higher you go. What feels like a stiff breeze in the valley can become a gale high in the hills, making the going harder than expected. Expecting two to three times the wind speed on the summits to that at sea level is a useful rule of thumb. Wind speeds on the summit of Ben Nevis average three times those in Fort William for example.

Narrowings within the hills also accelerate the wind. The commonest example of this being a col between two summits or a steep sided valley. Even though lower in height, the wind is often stronger in a col than on the tops.

If a general forecast says it will be quite breezy, then you may want to think twice before heading out on an exposed ridge. The good thing is that wind tends to come from a specific direction, and picking routes on a hill's sheltered side should result in the wind's full strength being avoided until near the summit.

Temperature

You don't need to be a genius to conclude that it gets colder the higher you get. This is because air cools with altitude, dry air at about 1°C per 100 metres and moist or foggy air half as quickly, at about 1°C per 200 metres. If the TV forecast says that North Wales will experience a clear day, with Bangor at a respectable 10°C, then the summit of Snowdon could be a chilly zero. Brrrrrrr!!

The combined effect of wind and temperature should also be considered. Wind chill is a major mountain hazard in the UK, and a common contributory factor in hypothermia cases. Cold air combined with a strong wind can result in it feeling much colder, and the body cooling quickly. Some mountain specific weather forecasts, such as those produced by the Mountain Weather Information Service, provide wind chill indications.

Precipitation

Most of our weather comes from the south west in the form of moist warm air that has travelled over the Atlantic. When it hits the mountains this air is forced upwards and cools with the moisture condensing into water droplets. The common situation of a clear valley floor and cloud covered summits is the clearest example of this phenomenon. As the air gets pushed even higher, the moisture forms droplets that fall back down to earth as rain.

Warm moist air rising, cooling and forming clouds

Added to the mix is Britain's location on the boundary between a cold air mass over the Arctic and a warmer one further south. Britain receives much warm and wet south westerly air which has travelled from the Gulf of Mexico, the so called Gulf Stream. On meeting the colder Arctic air, the warm air rises forming weather depressions. This results in our predominantly wet weather.

When thinking what weather to expect, consider the direction of the prevailing wind given in a forecast. This will help you to predict the characteristics of any weather systems that are carried by that wind.

To the north and west of Britain are oceans and so northerly and westerly air flows commonly bring precipitation. South and east of Britain is mainly land, and wind from those directions will generally be drier. South of Britain is also warm, and so is the wind. And there are no prizes for guessing that northerlies are cold as they originate in the Arctic.

The only 'odd' winds are easterlies. They are usually drier than those which track over the sea, but reflecting the land they pass over, are biting cold in winter yet can be quite balmy in summer.

Combined weather effects

Together, cold temperatures, rain and wind can create a sense of anxiety and urgency. This may lead to hurried and unconsidered decisions being made. Good planning should predict the likelihood of these conditions and allow some critical decisions to be made in advance.

In winter, wind direction is an important factor when it comes to slopes becoming avalanche prone. A south westerly wind can pick up snow from windward slopes and deposit it on north easterly leeward slopes. This can lead to unstable wind slab snowpacks being created. Read Chapter 5 for more about this topic.

The weather can affect your rate of travel. If the wind is strong then having it behind you is going to make the going much quicker than fighting against it. Poor visibility will require more detailed navigation, which will take time. It is possible to encounter snow and ice in autumn, spring and winter, and if met unexpectedly, may necessitate a detour. Finally, it is not always cold and wet; sometimes it can be too warm. On hot summer days take your time, use sun protection and drink plenty of liquid as heatstroke and dehydration are extremely debilitating.

In summary, understanding how weather 'works', paying attention to forecasts, being ready for abrupt changes, being well equipped and able to navigate if caught out, will all go towards reducing the risks posed by Britain's mountain weather.

ANIMALS

As well as the three hazards already covered, some thought should be given to animals. The bears, wolves and wild boar that were once indigenous to our Isles were hunted to extinction many centuries ago. In their place, the mysterious big cats of Bodmin Moor are the only large carnivorous mammals running wild. Two real hazards are far less dramatic however, the humble cow and the terrible tick!

Cows

People have been attacked or trampled to death by cows whilst quietly walking their dog. Most members of the public are wary of bulls, but few realise that cows, particularly those protecting newly-born calves, can also be dangerous. So what should you do?

In these reported cases, the cows are thought to have been trying to drive off the dogs in order to protect their young. While such attacks are relatively rare, Health and Safety Executive figures show that over 60 people are injured by cows each year.

The countryside is a great place to exercise dogs, but it is every owner's duty to make sure their dog is not a danger or nuisance to farm animals, wildlife or other people.

Moo-ve away!

By law, farmers are entitled to destroy a dog that injures or worries their animals, therefore dog walkers should keep their dogs on their lead at any time of the year when near farm animals, particularly during the lambing season. However, it is really important to be aware that there will be circumstances when you should release your dog from its lead.

Keep calm, carry on…
If walking a dog and you find yourself in a field of wary cattle, move away as carefully and quietly as possible, and if you feel threatened by cattle release your dog from its lead. Let it run free rather than try to protect it, endangering you. The dog will outrun both the cows and you. Leaving the lead attached to the collar poses a strangulation risk for the dog.

Those without canine companions should follow similar advice: move away calmly, do not panic and make no sudden noises. Chances are the cows will

Keep your dog under control

leave you alone once they establish that you pose no threat. If you walk through a field of cows and there happen to be calves, then try to choose a different route to avoid them.

Ticks
There's nothing quite like discovering a tick on your body to make you squirm. Knowing that it is contentedly feeding on your blood the natural instinct is to rip it out immediately, but wait. Tick borne diseases are on the rise in many hill walking areas – stack the odds in your favour by removing the tick properly.

Ticks are small arachnids, about the size of a poppy seed. They are external parasites that live off the blood of birds and mammals – including you. They are second only to mosquitoes for carrying diseases to humans, and in Britain can carry Lyme disease.

Ticks live in the soil and emerge to climb tall grass, shrubs, bushes and low level tree branches up to a height of 20 – 70cm in search of a blood host. They attack when you, or an animal, brush past and look for an area of soft skin into which they can insert their feeding organ.

They can attach themselves almost anywhere but prefer dark creases like the armpit, groin and back of the knee. You won't feel a thing, as the tick injects a toxin to anaesthetise the bite area and once embedded they will steadily engorge as they feed on your blood. They can also leave you with a nasty farewell present.

Lyme disease is caused by a bacteria carried by ticks in many popular British and European walking areas. But do not panic, being bitten by a tick does not mean you will contract Lyme disease. However carry out a body check if you go bushwhacking as soon as possible and use either a specialist tool or fine pair of tweezers to remove any ticks you find.

To reduce the chance of the tick injecting its infected stomach contents into you, the most important thing to remember when removing a tick is not to squeeze its body. Therefore, do not use your fingers to pull it out.

The most famous symptom of Lyme disease is a bullseye rash consisting of a red ring-shaped rash which gradually spreads from the site of the tick bite, usually with a fading centre. It's like a browny-red or pink expanding polo mint. It appears 2 – 40 days after infection and is the only sure-fire symptom of Lyme disease. If you develop one take a photo immediately to show your doctor in case it disappears.

Less than 50% of people with Lyme disease get this rash. If Lyme disease is left untreated a whole range of symptoms can develop, including a flu-like illness, facial palsy, viral-type meningitis, arthritic-like joint pains, nerve inflammation, disturbance of sensation or clumsiness of movement and encephalitis (swelling of the brain).

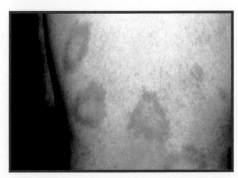

Bullseye rash

Removing a tick with fine ended tweezers and specialist tools

If you suspect you have Lyme disease then head straight to your GP. A blood test is available, but if your GP suspects Lyme, they should begin antibiotic treatment right away, without waiting for the results.

Prevention is better than cure and taking steps to prevent tick bites is the best plan to follow.

• Avoid unnecessary bushwacking and walk in the middle of paths.

• Keep your arms and legs covered. Light coloured fabrics are useful since the ticks stand out.

• Check clothes and skin frequently.

• Ideally, do a buddy check every 3 – 4 hours. Ticks are large enough to be easily spotted in summer, but you need to look carefully in spring; they can be very small.

• Check that ticks are not brought home on clothes and pets.

• Check children carefully, especially along the hairline and scalp.

• Do a thorough full body check within 24 hours of being out on the hill.

• Where possible, use an effective tool and technique to get ticks out.

• Do not use heat, Vaseline or other creams to suffocate the tick, this could increase the risk of infection.

For more information watch the tick awareness film on both the *Hill Walking Essentials* DVD and the BMC website at **www.thebmc.co.uk/ticks**

CHAPTER 4

NAVIGATION

Effective navigation not only helps to make you safer on the hill, it can also mean a better day out. Develop navigation skills incrementally on less serious hills in good weather, before choosing more challenging objectives.

Don't get lost!

If new to hill walking be aware that poor navigation skills (or a complete lack of them!) are a very common contributory factor in mountain incidents attended by Mountain Rescue Teams. Straying into steep or serious terrain can result in getting stuck and being unable to get down unassisted, or slipping and becoming injured.

Map reading vs navigation

It's useful to draw a distinction between map reading and navigation, as they are often confused as the same thing. Map reading could be described as understanding the different map symbols and topographical features. Knowing that blue symbols are wet, for example, or that the distance between contour lines tells you how steep a slope is. Navigation is very different and is the ability to use this information effectively. This includes planning a route or being able to use the map to find your way.

Maps

In Britain the most commonly used maps for hill walking are Ordnance Survey maps in either 1:50,000 or 1:25,000 scale and Harvey Maps in either 1:40,000 or 1:25,000 scale. The 1:40,000 British Mountain Maps use Harvey mapping and cover the most popular walking destinations in Britain. Made from waterproof and tear resistant plastic they are both light and durable.

Large scale 1:25,000 maps can be useful when navigating in complex areas such as the margins of open country where walls and fences abound, or where detailed micro-navigation is essential. Small scale 1:50,000 maps make route planning easier as they convey the ground shape without a lot of additional information. They are also a wise choice in winter when much of the detail on large scale maps lies under a blanket of snow. Lying in between these scales, 1:40,000 maps cover large enough areas for route planning and yet display enough detail when precise navigation is required. Developing the ability to work with different scales is important.

The map has to be waterproof or contained in a waterproof map case – a wet and soggy map is a liability. Fold the map so that you can see the relevant area while still being able to fit it into a jacket pocket. It's important to be able to put the map away but also get it out again easily so have a pocket reserved especially for your map. An elastic band can be used to keep the map compact.

Grids, scales and distances

British maps have a gridline system superimposed upon them. These grids represent one-kilometre squares regardless of the map scale, and can be used as a useful rough measure when planning a route. Grid north is the northerly direction of the north/south grid lines, and is different to magnetic north, the direction that a compass needle points to.

Waterproof British Mountain Maps cover many popular walking areas

The grid lines are numbered and most maps include instructions on how to work out a grid reference which describes a unique 100m by 100m square on the map. It is wise to spend some time making sure you know how to do this before heading for the hills, as a grid reference is needed should you need to pass your location onto someone else, such as a Mountain Rescue Team.

When you know the scale of a map you can use a ruler to measure the distance between two points and then convert this to a distance on the ground. On 1:25,000 maps, 4mm is equivalent to 100m on the ground; on 1:40,000 maps, 2.5mm is equivalent to 100m on the ground; and on 1:50,000 maps, 2mm is equivalent to 100m on the ground.

Getting started

In this section, we will concentrate on some of the most important navigation skills, namely: setting the map, contour interpretation, tick-off and catching features, using the compass, estimating distance, route choice and relocation strategies. The Global Positioning System or GPS is also covered. For a more visual explanation of these skills in action watch the Navigation chapter of the *Hill Walking Essentials* DVD which complements much of this book, or read *Navigation in the Mountains*, published by Mountain Leader Training.

SETTING THE MAP

This is positioning the map so that all the features are lined up, with your location as the central point. What is in front of you on the ground will be in front of you on the map, what is to your left on the ground will be to your left on the map, and so on.

It does not matter if the map is upside down, as you do not need to read the text. Instead, you need to read the map symbols, lining them up with the features you can see. Rotate the map to keep it set when you change direction. In good visibility you should be able to set the map by eye, using obvious features such as a hill top or major track junction.

In poor visibility, you can set the map by lining up the compass needle with any of the north/south grid lines. Make sure that the north end of the needle, which is often painted red, points towards the top of the map, otherwise you will set your map 180° in the wrong direction!

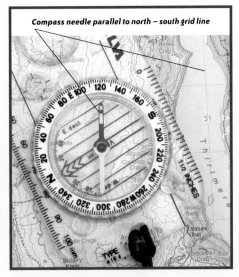

Compass needle parallel to north – south grid line

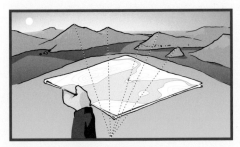

Setting the map using landscape features

Setting the map using the compass

CONTOUR INTERPRETATION

Navigating in urban areas using man-made features such as roads and buildings is common to us all. If you get lost, there is always something nearby like a street name to set you back on course. It is not so easy in the uplands, as man-made features are not always reliable, or even present. Paths can be confusing, as they may not always be marked, and even watercourses can change if it has been very dry, or more commonly, very wet!

For these reasons the contour lines remain the most useful feature on the map to describe the terrain both near and far. Once you can interpret the contours you're well placed to explore Britain's uplands.

What is a contour?

A contour is a line that links land of equal height. Contours are measured in metres above sea level and shown on the map as lines printed with a set interval between them. Ordnance Survey maps commonly use a 10m contour interval and British Mountain Maps use a 15m contour interval. The actual height of a contour, such as 150m, will be marked periodically to help when navigating.

Contours are used to represent the three dimensional world on a two dimensional map, and it can be hard to 'read the contours' at first. To help, imagine a three tiered wedding cake, each tier holding a cake wrapped in a purple band. Viewed side on you would see three bands, one above the other, each narrower than the one below. Viewed from above you would see three purple circles, one inside the other, with the sense of height between the tiers being lost.

Using this analogy, the map is like the bird's eye view, in which we see contour 'bands' around the hills on a flat map. But when walking in the hills they are anything but flat! The skill to develop is converting the information given by the contours into a three dimensional image in your mind.

This may sound complicated, but the good news is that there are in fact only six general contour features to interpret:

i) Ring contours

The clue is in the name with these ones – they are literally a ring or circle. Ring contours portray a hill top or piece of high ground. When stood in

The relationship between contours and a hill

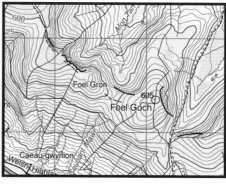

Ring contours describing the summits of Foel Gron and Foel Goch

the middle of a ring contour all the land around you will be falling away, and on the map the contour will connect to itself, like a ring.

ii) Cols, saddles, and bwlchs

Often situated between two summits, cols are very common features in the hills. When stood on a col with the land rising up to your sides, the land in front and behind you will drop away. This is the same shape as a horse's saddle which rises up at the front and back, and drops away on either side.

Cols can be very conclusive features to navigate to, with the contours on the maps making them clear to identify. Bwlch is Welsh for col, and knowing Gaelic or Welsh terms for common mountain features can help when navigating.

iii) Slopes

Slopes give us two useful pieces of information: the steepness of the slope and the direction, or aspect, it faces. As a slope steepens the contours become closer together on the map, and as a slope shallows, the contours become wider apart.

A slope that becomes progressively shallower as you climb is called a convex slope. A characteristic of such a slope is thinking you're near the top, only for more of the hill to come into view. A slope that becomes progressively steeper as you climb is called a concave slope. These are common in the hills, where glaciers have carved out valleys.

iv) Ridges

Ridges define many of our iconic mountains, often forming a natural line to follow. Contours form V shapes around ridges, with the point of the V marking the crest of the ridge. Ridges can also be very steep on each side, but relatively flat to follow, such as Crib Goch. In those cases, there will be two slopes on either side, which meet at the ridge crest.

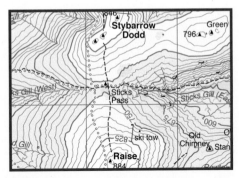

Sticks Pass: a col between Stybarrow Dodd and Raise

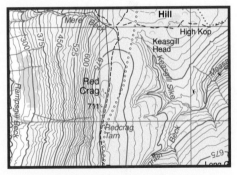

A steep westerly slope and shallow easterly slope on either side of Red Crag

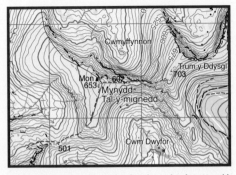

North westerly and south easterly ridges descending from Mynydd-Tal-y-mignedd and Trum y Ddysgl

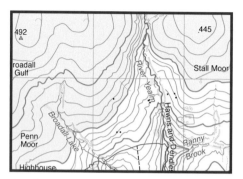

Two valleys

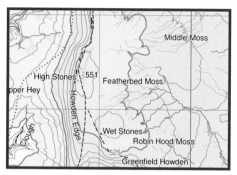

Featherbed moss: very flat!

v) Valleys and re-entrants

Valleys come in a range of sizes, and as with ridges, they are described by a V shape in the contours, with the point of the V marking the bottom of the valley. A dry valley is often called a re-entrant, the reason for such an odd word is that the contours describing it 're-enter' the hillside, so to speak, but have no water course running through them. Re-entrants are generally either a single contour, or a few contours long.

It can sometimes be difficult to decide whether V shaped contours depict a ridge or a valley. If the contour heights increase in the direction to which the V points, then the feature is a valley. If the contour heights decrease in the direction to which the V points, then the feature is a ridge. One final clue: if there is a watercourse at the point of the V, it is definitely a valley!

vi) Flat areas

Though not strictly a contour feature, the notable absence of contours means that the area is flat. Hills are hilly, so flat areas can be very useful features to navigate by. A col, for example, can be thought of as a flat area in the middle of land that is rising up on two opposite sides, and dropping away on another two.

Reading the contours

The best way to develop contour interpretation skills is in good weather. When it comes to contours, even on poor weather days you could explore enclosed valley bases, which are often full of little knolls and small re-entrants. Alternatively, when following a well defined path, match up the changes in steepness with the contour features on the map. If you notice an obvious knoll, ridge or re-entrant nearby, identify the corresponding contour feature on the map. Ticking off features in this way, helps you to keep tabs on where you are on the map.

When walking in the hills, the terrain and views constantly change in shape, aspect and gradient, all of which are described by the contours. Add to your mental 'image library' how the contours on the map match up with the features you see each time you head out. This will help you navigate when the chips are down!

TICK-OFF AND CATCHING FEATURES

Identifying both tick-off and catching features allows you to continually monitor where you are.

As mentioned earlier, urban navigation skills translate well to the mountains and tick-off and catching features are two obvious examples. For example, the instructions to get to someone's house could be, "Follow the road to the Post Office, turn left, take the second path on the right and follow this to the house with the red door. If you pass the church you've gone too far."

In this example, the Post Office and path junctions are tick-off features, waymarking the journey, and the Church is a catching feature, highlighting the need to stop and turn around. Such urban navigation is often carried out using features identified by someone else, but when hill walking, you need to identify features on the map yourself. When planning your route, identify features you can tick-off as you walk, and which will catch you if you stray off course.

Imagine walking from Fairfield to Hart Crag. The path from Fairfield summit is flat at first, going south east for a short distance. The path then bends east and gently downhill. It then turns one final time, heading south east and down to the col called Link Hause, before climbing up to Hart Crag.

Path bends are not always obvious, and it can be easy to miss them. Over shooting the first bend would lead into the steep downhill slopes of Nettle Cove, as opposed to the gentle downhill of the path. This quick steepening of the slope would therefore be an obvious catching feature, highlighting that the first path bend had been missed.

If the second path bend were overshot, a walker would find themselves above the cliff called Scrubby Crag. This abrupt change from flat to vertical is another catching feature.

There are also numerous tick-off features between the two summits: the two path bends; the gentle downhill section in the path heading east from Fairfield; a small ring contour, before the path begins to bend south; the drop down to the col at Link Hause; Link Hause itself; and the final rise up to Hart Crag.

Going through such a mental exercise **before** setting off creates an expectation of what should be encountered en route. If all goes to plan, then great. But if something unexpected turns up, you will be less likely to go too far off route as alarm bells should ring.

It is worth noting that in the example above, all but two of the tick-off and catching features are contour features: changes in the steepness of terrain, a ring contour and a col. This serves to emphasise the importance of developing good contour interpretation skills.

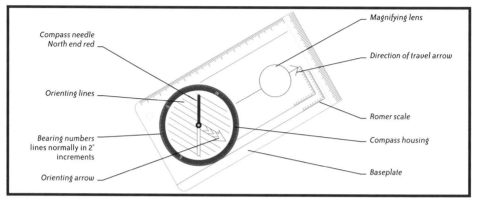

Compass needle
North end red

Orienting lines

Bearing numbers
lines normally in 2°
increments

Orienting arrow

Magnifying lens

Direction of travel arrow

Romer scale

Compass housing

Baseplate

A typical hill walking compass

THE COMPASS

A hill walking compass will have a large baseplate
to make it easier to handle and take bearings,
especially when wearing gloves or mitts,
a magnifying glass, measuring romer scales
and rubber feet for gripping the map.

You also need a way of attaching the compass so
you won't lose it when you let go. Compasses are
commonly worn around the neck, but you could
also attach it elsewhere.

The compass performs several tasks. It is used for
measuring bearings and distances on the map and
for following magnetic bearings when walking.

Taking and walking on a bearing

Before taking a bearing, always estimate visually
what the bearing will be. You can then check this
against the bearing taken with the compass to
make sure you have not made a basic error.
In the four diagrams opposite, the leg is roughly
north east.

With the magnetic bearing set, hold the compass
close to your chest and look down onto it. Rotate
you body until the north end of magnetic needle

Sighting a feature with a compass

is aligned with the north end of the orienting arrow.
Now look up to see where you are headed. Holding
the compass in this way ensures your body faces the
direction you need to walk.

Next, identify a feature which lies on the bearing.
It might be a rock or a clump of vegetation, and
once identified, there is no need to use the compass
again until you have reached it. You can take any
route around obstacles to get to the feature. It is
essential to maintain your fix on the feature as
it may change in appearance the closer you get.

How to take a bearing

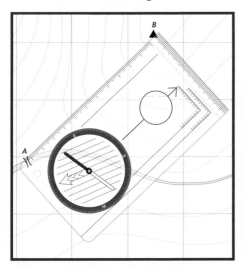

A Align the compass along the required route on the map

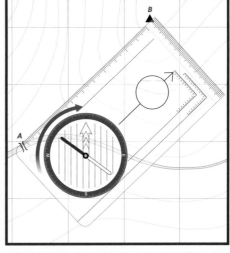

B Rotate the compass housing to align the orientating lines with the north-south grid lines on the map

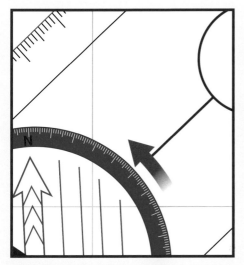

C Rotate the compass housing to compensate for magnetic variation

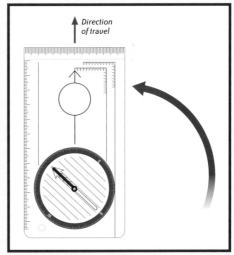

D Remove the compass from the map, rotate the compass so that the north end of the needle and the orientating arrow are aligned and then proceed following the direction of travel arrow

Once you reach the first feature, repeat the exercise until the whole leg is completed. The features chosen need to be between you and your final destination.

If walking on a bearing is new to you, why not practise in your local park or when out walking on a sunny day? It is best to feel comfortable with navigation skills before having to use them for real.

ESTIMATING DISTANCE

As important a skill as walking on a bearing is being able to estimate the distance you have travelled. Pacing and timing can help with this and the first stage is measuring the distance on the map, which is done using the millimetre or romer scales on the compass baseplate. The romer scales reduce the likelihood of making a error when converting something measured on a map to the distance you expect to walk – as long as use the right scale! Silva Type 4 Expedition compasses have three romers for the three common map scales.

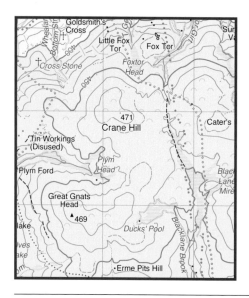

Pacing

Estimating distance by pacing requires knowing how many double paces you walk to 100m. To establish how many double paces you walk for 100m, identify a 100m flat stretch on a map with identifiable markers at each end, such as wall junctions, or use a measured distance, such as a running track. Depending upon stride length most people walk between 60 and 80 double paces. Pacing works best for short distances, up to 500m; is counted in hundred metre blocks; and is used when there is an absence of tick-off features. Dartmoor is one upland area where there can be few navigation features. Imagine walking east for 500m from Crane Hill to meet the path running north – south. In poor visibility, walking in a straight line on a bearing is the logical strategy to follow, and pacing could be used to estimate the distance travelled and ensure the path is not overshot.

If you walked 64 double paces per hundred metres, then after 64 paces you would start again at zero and walk a second 64 paces. And so on until you completed this five times.

It's important to realise that pacing is only estimation. With only a 5% error in the previous example you could be 25m short. Therefore, when using pacing don't expect to arrive exactly at your destination, but if accurate, you should be very close. When walking uphill, in deep snow or on uneven ground pacing will be less accurate. It's important to bear this in mind.

Timing

Put simply, if you know the speed you walk, you can estimate the distance travelled. Reasonably fit people walk at 4 or 5 kilometres per hour, and the chart below shows how long it would take to walk up to 1km at different speeds. It is usual to add up to one minute for every 10 metres of ascent, but when going downhill, you can usually ignore the height loss and only use the time for the horizontal distance.

When using timing a stop watch works best as you can stop the clock when you take a break.

In the pacing example, timing could also have been used to measure the 500m travelled. Once you have tried both timing and pacing, you will be best placed to decide which one to use in different situations. As a general rule, timing works best when a steady walking pace can be maintained and a long distance is being walked. Pacing can be very useful over short distances when precision is required.

ROUTE CHOICE

Being able to choose an appropriate route and then follow it using the skills outlined in this chapter is the sign of a competent navigator.

Urban navigation skills translate well to the mountains, the use of tick-off and catching features being two obvious examples. Urban navigation is carried out using familiar pointers, such as buildings. In the hills you have to use the map to identify pointers you think you will be able to find easily.

Here we're looking at a journey from Garnedd Gwenllian (A) to a small sheep fold (B).

Going in a straight line is unlikely to prove successful especially if the mist comes down. The distance is 1½ kilometres and this is a long way to stay on track with few prominent features along the route. A steep crag would also be passed just above the sheep fold. A route avoiding this hazard would be preferable.

Distance travelled metres	Speed kilometres per hour			
	5	4	3	2
1000m	12 min	15 min	20 min	30 min
800m	10 min	12 min	16 min	24 min
700m	9 min	11 min	14 min	21 min
500m	6 min	7½ min	10 min	15 min
400m	5 min	6 min	8 min	12 min
200m	2½ min*	3 min	4 min	6 min
100m	1¼ min*	1½ min	2 min	3 min

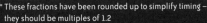

* These fractions have been rounded up to simplify timing – they should be multiples of 1.2

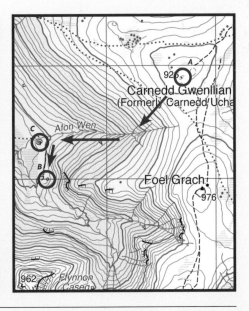

The route marked is slightly longer in distance but more likely to be successful as it consists of three shorter legs. Prominent tick-off and catching features have been chosen which can be identified along the way.

Leaving Garnedd Gwenllian on a south westerly bearing, leads to a stream after 700m, which can then be followed downhill. Even if the stream was not obvious, the very prominent valley described by the contours would be very clear. On a more southerly bearing the top of the stream could be reached after only 400m, but with its bed poorly defined at that point, there is a chance of walking past and missing it. When heading for a long linear feature, such as a stream, aim for a point where you think it will be well defined, as shown by the contours in this case.

Following the stream down, the second tick-off feature is a significant change in the steepness of the ground, as the contours become more widely spaced, and the ground becomes almost flat. At this point it is necessary to walk southerly along a footpath.

If the path is missed, an obvious catching feature is reached in the form of a large circular sheep fold (C).

The final destination (B) could then be reached either by a short backtrack up the stream to find the path, or in poor visibility, on a compass bearing from the sheepfold, estimating the distance travelled using either pacing or timing.

Being able to select an appropriate route and then follow it using the other skills which have been outlined can be very satisfying, great fun, and most importantly will help you to have successful days out on the hill.

RELOCATION STRATEGIES

There is a difference between not having a clue where you are, and not knowing exactly where you are. The former can be avoided by periodically checking your position throughout the day, the latter happens to all walkers and mountaineers, and is not necessarily something to be concerned about.

By including catching features in your route planning you will go a long way to staying on track, as alarm bells should ring before you stray too far. If you still end up 'lost', stop and go through this mental exercise:

Where is your last known point?

This is an important reference point, and by using tick-off features en route, the answer is hopefully not 'the car park!'

What's happened since leaving your last known point?

If you've walked uphill then you have immediately cut out areas on the map lower than your last known point. Or if you walked steeply downhill and then flat, that too would be shown on the map by contours close together and then no contours at all. This is all really useful information to help you relocate.

When did you leave your last known point?

If you left this point only half an hour ago, then you are unlikely to have walked more than about 2 km. This may imply you have a large area to consider, but when combined with the previous question, relatively large parts of the map can be excluded as a possible location.

What's around you?

Consider what the land you can see would look like on the map, as the features will be marked on the map.

Make a plan

Let's assume that you're still not sure, or poor visibility makes your job more difficult. One option is to walk on a bearing for a set distance, on a sort of fact finding mission. The idea being to see what the terrain does – up, down or flat – and identify any obvious features you encounter. If that does not help, then retrace your steps back to the start point and repeat the exercise in another direction. This should help you build enough of a picture in your mind to identify your location on the map.

If all of this fails, then the best option may be to walk on a bearing in the direction which you think will take you to a 'safe area' where you can hopefully relocate more effectively.

Whatever strategy you choose, be methodical: walk on a bearing and estimate the distance you travel. Wandering around with no plan at all will just get you even more lost!

THE GLOBAL POSITIONING SYSTEM OR GPS

The Global Positioning System (GPS) can be a very useful navigation aid for hill walkers. It is important to recognise that using GPS receivers cannot be a substitute for the core navigation skills, especially contour interpretation and route choice.

The most tangible and obvious benefit of a GPS receiver is obtaining a grid reference of your position, a very useful aid if you have become disorientated or during an emergency. The ability to use grid references is vital because this is the only way you can translate the position which the GPS provides. Most hand-held receivers likely to be used by hill walkers have a specified accuracy to about 15 metres.

The GPS receiver needs to have a line of sight to at least four satellites and the more satellites it can access then the more accurate it will be. Anything which obstructs the line of sight will reduce accuracy. The obstruction might be a cliff, a steep sided valley or trees in a forest.

If you become lost remain calm and make a plan

Using a GPS receiver to fix a location

The GPS receiver has to be formatted to the correct time zone, map datum and position format for the map you are using, such as Greenwich Mean Time, Ordnance Survey and British Grid. For the last of these, the correct two letter prefix is required, which identifies the specific 100 kilometre square you are using. An easily made mistake is to forget that the letters change every time you reach the 00 grid numbers. This often occurs within one map sheet.

Another useful feature of GPS receivers is being able to enter the grid reference of a location you want to go to and then following the arrow on the receiver in much the same way as you would follow a compass bearing. As the GPS handset will take you in a straight line to your destination, you need to ensure that such a route will not lead you over a cliff edge or through other hazards.

Software is available which makes it easy to create routes. Once you have created a route on the mapping software, you can load it into your GPS receiver.

You should not become totally reliant on a GPS receiver, as you might run out of batteries or damage your receiver. Yet another reason why being able to navigate using a map and compass is such a vital hill walking skill.

CHAPTER 5

WALKING IN WINTER

Britain's mountains offer limitless adventure in winter. Remote and beautiful, they present exciting challenges for walkers and mountaineers alike. Moving around in the winter environment requires specific skills and equipment over and above those used in summer.

What is winter?

The hills and mountains can be snow and ice free over Christmas, but crampons and axes are often essential when climbing Ben Nevis in April. When venturing into the mountains in winter, the terrain underfoot is what's relevant, as this will impact most directly upon the skills you need to master.

In this chapter we cover what is required to cope with the various terrains and conditions encountered in winter. For comprehensive advice on all the topics covered here, watch the BMC *Winter Essentials* DVD or read *Winter Skills*, published by Mountain Leader Training.

EQUIPMENT

As it is colder in winter than summer you will need more clothes, but it is not quite as simple as that. On a cloud free day with the sun reflecting off the snow walking can become a very sweaty enterprise! If the sun disappears and the wind picks up it can then become bitterly cold in an instant. Just as in summer, a flexible clothing system is required, along with some extra insulating layers.

A hat, scarf (or fleece neck band) and gloves or mitts are essential bits of winter kit. Always take a spare pair of gloves/mitts too. If you lose one you can incapacitate your hands, or worse still, get frostbite.

As walking is more physical in winter, more energy is required than in summer. You will be surprised just how much food you can eat! Food can also freeze and leave you cracking a tooth if you're not careful. Taking on enough fluid is important too. A hot flask provides a welcome winter warmer and if possible, fill your water bottle with hot water too, to avoid it freezing.

To protect the face and eyes from wind blasted snow, double lens ski goggles should be taken. It is almost impossible to look forwards without goggles if snow is being blown into the face, so they should be thought of as a prerequisite, rather than an optional extra. Double lens goggles will mist up much less than single lens models, and the general rule is that once goggles are on the face, they should be left there until you need to take them off. Constantly removing them during use is likely to lead to them getting filled with snow, making it very hard to see. On clear days, sunglasses and sunscreen will protect the face and eyes.

Finally, with this extra food, fluid and clothing, plus goggles, crampons and ice axe, you will need a good sized rucksack between 40 and 50 litres to carry it all.

You need to eat lots when winter walking

Moving around

In a single day you could walk over a variety of terrain, including: unfrozen ground in the valleys; frozen soil and vegetation higher up; soft, hard packed or frozen snow; and patches of ice and ice covered rock. As mentioned in Chapter 2, a pair of winter boots is necessary as they will keep your feet warm and provide you with the required grip and support.

The points about movement skills noted in Chapter 3 are of even greater importance in winter as the consequences of a slip can be more serious. The good news is that winter boots provide a lot of support, allowing you to kick steps in frozen snow or ground effectively. Walking poles are commonly used in winter to provide extra stability, but on steeper ground an axe should be held. Unlike poles, an axe can be used to self arrest should you slip.

In winter, you need to be prepared for sudden changes in terrain. A patch of ice on a path or a small section of deep soft snow could catch you unawares. The need for good movement skills in winter is also made apparent by the fact that you can leave a relatively safe spot for one with real objective danger in only a few footsteps. Feel confident moving around in summer first, and then progressively develop your movement skills in winter.

ICE AXE

An axe is a vital piece of winter equipment and has a variety of functions; here we will look at using it for support and to stop you should you slip.

When walking on steeper terrain the axe is held in the uphill hand to provide support. You should always get your axe out on flat terrain before you actually need it. If zig-zagging up a slope, you will

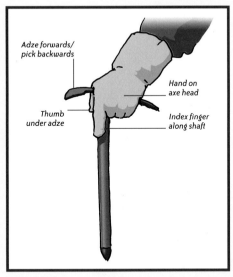

Adze forwards/
pick backwards

Hand on
axe head

Thumb
under adze

Index finger
along shaft

Holding an ice axe

need to change the hand holding the axe each time you change direction. For this reason, do not attach a leash to your wrist, but remove it from the axe before setting off. Leaving a leash dangling down to get caught up in your feet is not an option!

A leash is commonly used when the axe is being swung to cut a step with the adze, or make a placement with the pick. Using a leash when walking may provide a feeling of extra security, but the need to provide real security on steep slopes or complex ridges by regularly switching the axe between hands means that a leash is best not used in those situations.

As for the length of your axe, when holding the head in your hand, the spike should be level with your boot top. A walking axe is usually between 60 and 65cm long.

CRAMPONS

Crampons are attached to your boots for safer travel over hard packed snow or ice. Apart from knowing how to use them effectively, what is most important is ensuring the crampons are compatible with your boots, and then fitting them properly. If you get this wrong, the crampons will not work, making walking more difficult, or they may simply fall off unexpectedly. Both scenarios are potentially very hazardous.

For the purpose of ensuring that boots and crampons are compatible, boots are rated B0, B1, B2 and B3. Of the three broad boot types discussed in Chapter 2, approach shoes equate to B0, hill walking boots to B1, and mountaineering boots to B2 and B3.

B0: Not recommended for crampons.

B1: Suitable for the easiest snow and ice conditions found when hill walking. Crampons are likely to be used in an emergency when crossing short sections of snow or ice.

B2: A stiff flex boot designed for mountain use and could be used all day with crampons.

B3: A rigid climbing/mountaineering boot, suitable for crampons.

Crampons are similarly categorised C1, C2 and C3.

C1: A flexible walking crampon attached with straps. With or without front points.

C2: Articulated multi-purpose crampons with front points. Attached with straps all round or straps at the front and clip-on heel.

C3: Articulated or fully rigid technical crampon attached by full clip-on system at toe and heel.

Make sure you can attach your crampons when wearing gloves

In a nutshell, the stiffer the boot, the greater the variety of crampon types it can take.

Boot Rating	Compatible Crampon Type
B0	None
B1	C1
B2	C1 – C2
B3	C1 – C2 – C3

Walking in crampons

When you first try it, walking in crampons is surprisingly difficult. It is easy to trip up, spike your own leg or tear your gaiters. When not wearing crampons on steep slopes of hard frozen snow, the boot edge is used to cut a flat platform to stand on. Conversely, when wearing crampons on such slopes the ankle should be rotated to keep the foot flat on the snow. This will ensure that the crampon points dig in and gain purchase. This is known as flat-footing.

The following tips should help:

- Keep your feet flat to the snow or ice.

- In wet snow, crampons collect compacted snow between the points, known as balling up. Stop excessive build-up by tapping the crampons with the axe to free the snow.

- Develop a walking style where your feet are further apart. Take short steps.

- Avoid baggy overtrousers or loose gaiters which are easy to catch with your crampons as you walk.

Get used to your crampons on relatively non-testing ground. It is better to stumble and trip on the valley floor on the approach to a hillside, than to find yourself gripped by the unfamiliarity of your footwear in a serious situation.

It is all too tempting to delay putting on crampons until they are really needed – at which point it is invariably difficult to do! Anticipate where you will need your crampons and make sure you have already strapped them to your feet in advance.

You will be better prepared if you practice putting your crampons on at home in the garden; and wear your gloves whilst doing this. You could even get used to walking in them up and down a steep

Flexing the ankle to flat-foot on frozen snow

grassy slope with you ice axe. You may get some odd looks, but such preparation is worth it!

WINTER WEATHER

The need to obtain a weather forecast goes without saying, but if heading out for the first time you are unlikely to be aware of how extreme winter weather can be. Unlike the summer, when it is possible to battle on in all but the most severe of situations, winter weather can quite literally stop you in your tracks. The wind can be so strong as to blow you over, a potentially very serious situation if walking on a steep slope or ridge. Needless to say, a forecast will help you plan your day appropriately.

When the mist comes down in summer, it is still possible to get information from the ground around you, but this is not the case with full snow cover. With everything white, the horizon disappears making it impossible to gauge even the steepness of the ground in front of you.

WINTER NAVIGATION

Navigating in winter is more difficult than in summer for two main reasons. Firstly, snow cover can hide many features, such as streams, ponds, walls and paths, and with snow accumulating in hollows and lee slopes, the ground can appear different to what you may expect from the map's contours.

The second challenge is the nature of the winter environment itself. In poor visibility with the wind blowing snow into your face accurate navigation is vital. If you are unable to operate wearing gloves and goggles in such conditions, you will not be able to navigate effectively.

Finally, the consequences of poor navigation cannot be ignored. In summer, if you make an error, you are unlikely to walk off a cliff edge, as you will most likely see the drop first. Not so in winter when white-out conditions or a cornice can obscure your view. Before exploring the winter hills, sharpen up on your summer navigation.

This is the briefest of summaries on winter navigation, for more information read either *Winter Skills* or *Navigation in the Mountains*, both published by Mountain Leader Training.

Paths can become buried in snow

Winter navigation can be extremely testing

SELF BELAY AND SELF ARREST

Anyone who has tobogganed will know how quickly you can slide down even a gentle snow slope. Serious consequences can result from a slip in winter, such as falling over an edge, or getting slammed into a boulder field. The axe can be used to stop you in two different ways.

Self belay is a technique that can stop a slip becoming a slide. Very simply, should you lose your footing, applying your weight over the head of the axe will push it further into the snow, providing a 'belay' for you to grab hold of with the free hand. The feet should also be kicked into the snow.

Should you end up sliding down a slope, the axe can be used to bring you to a stop. It is not possible to go into great detail in this book, and all that is shown is the basic self arrest braking position to adopt. When you actually slip, you could slide head or feet first, on your front or on your back. There are established techniques to get the body into the braking position, and a film demonstrating self arrest can be viewed at **www.thebmc.co.uk/selfarrest**

Self belay and self arrest skills should be practiced on a slope with a safe run-out. In other words, if you fail to stop yourself, you will come to a natural rest in a safe place. When practicing, helmets should be worn and crampons taken off.

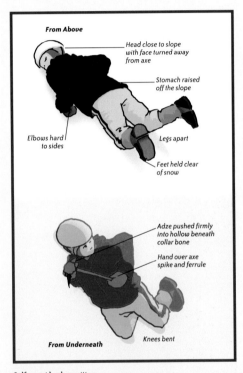

From Above

Head close to slope with face turned away from axe

Stomach raised off the slope

Elbows hard to sides

Legs apart

Feet held clear of snow

Adze pushed firmly into hollow beneath collar bone

Hand over axe spike and ferrule

From Underneath

Knees bent

Self arrest body position

Move body above axe head to push axe vertically into snow

Move arm round to hold base of shaft at snow level

Kick feet into slope

How to self belay

WINTER HAZARDS

Some winter hazards have already been highlighted, here we will go into a bit more detail on identifying and managing them.

Steep slopes

Slipping on a steep slope is obviously best avoided in summer or winter, so the first question to ask is, 'Can your route avoid steep slopes?' If the answer is no, then are all the people in your group able and equipped to tackle such obstacles? Having the right kit is only part of the solution, as possessing good movement skills should be the deciding factor. Secondly, is everyone able to arrest their fall should they slip? If the answer is no, then either spend some time practicing such skills or more preferably, take a different route.

Cornices

A cornice is an overhanging bank of snow projecting over the edge of a ridge or plateau. Formed by the wind depositing snow on lee slopes, they are extremely serious hazards. Cornices obscure cliff edges, and can collapse under your weight, resulting in a fatal fall. When walking on any snow-covered plateau or ridge, take great care when near a steep drop. Do not go as near the edge as you might in summer, as cornices can fracture some way back from the edge. Thawing conditions – rapid rises in temperature – will make cornices more unstable, so care should also be taken when walking underneath them.

Frozen water

Every winter, streams, ponds and lakes will freeze over in the mountains and become covered in snow. Many may be safe to cross, but if the ice or a snow bridge collapses under your weight, you could at best get wet and at worst be at risk from developing hypothermia or even drown. Good navigation should help you identify where watercourses lie, allowing you to negotiate them.

Cornices can obscure cliff edges: stay well back!

Avalanches

When the force of gravity on a snow slope exceeds the force of the anchors holding the snow in place an avalanche will occur, resulting in a mass of snow sliding downhill. Walkers get killed in avalanches, and so the seriousness of getting caught in one cannot be overstated. The chilling statistic is that around 90% of victims triggered the avalanched that engulfed them. There are a variety of avalanche types, and here we will look at the type most common to Britain – slab avalanches.

The snowpack in our hills is often made of discrete layers of snow, each formed by the wind compacting the snow into a slab. Because each slab is formed at different times and in different conditions, these resulting layers are often poorly bonded to each other. This creates instabilities in the whole snowpack.

Imagine such a layered snowpack on a slope. If more weight is applied, either in the form of more snow or a walker, then the bonds holding a layer (or layers) together could fail, resulting in a slab avalanche.

The first step to avoid being avalanched is to identify slopes where the snowpack could be unstable. Most slab avalanches occur on slopes angled between 30° and 45°, and just knowing this helps when considering your route for the day. Past and current weather forecasts provide an indication of recent and future snowfall, and the direction of the prevailing wind. If there has been lots of recent snow with a south westerly wind, for example, then northerly through to easterly slopes are likely to be loaded with snow.

The second step to avoid being avalanched is to choose a route avoiding slopes where the snowpack is unstable. This may sound obvious, but it is all too easy to get caught out by inadvertently straying into hazardous terrain, especially in poor visibility.

The sportscotland Avalanche Information Service (SAIS) provides Avalanche Hazard Reports for the popular walking and climbing areas in Scotland. These can be viewed or downloaded at **www.sais.gov.uk**. The website also provides further information on avalanche avoidance and top tips for identifying avalanche prone slopes. Even if you do not get to explore the Scottish hills in winter (which would be a shame!) the site is well worth a visit.

Full depth avalanche in Coire an Lochan

Slab breaking up under walking boots

CHAPTER 6

CAMPING IN THE HILLS

Spending a night in a tent can be an unforgettable experience – and hopefully a positive one! A multi-day trip in the hills, carrying all you require in a rucksack provides a great sense of freedom and with careful planning is relatively straightforward to achieve.

WHERE TO CAMP

In a valley with road access use a recognised campsite, as you should only wild camp if high in the hills, away from civilisation. Camping by the side of the road to save some money on campsite fees is not a good idea for a number of reasons.

First of all, wild camping is not permitted by right on open access land in England and Wales without express permission of the landowner, but it is permitted in Scotland on the proviso that you follow the *Scottish Outdoor Access Code (SOAC)* and provided that you do so responsibly as explained in SOAC. Popular valleys have enough pressure put upon them already, without the addition of unregulated camping by the side of a road, where appropriate sanitation facilities are unlikely to be available. Campsites also provide vital income to the rural economy.

When high in the hills the legal situation is the same as in the valleys, but your impact can be more easily managed. Before moving on to these environmental aspects some consideration will first be given to equipment and general backpacking tips.

Cook in the tent's porch

CAMPING EQUIPMENT

Over and above the equipment described in Chapter 2 a basic camping kit list includes:

- Tent or bivi bag

- Sleeping bag

- Sleeping mat

- Stove

- Pans & cutlery

- Water container

- Trowel (for disposal of human waste)

- More food!

- Appropriate rucksack

For an overnight camping trip high in the hills you are likely to need a rucksack of at least 50 litres capacity. Some people may take much larger sacks, but whatever size you take, human nature is such that you are likely to fill it! Therefore, think carefully about how large a sack you would feel happy to carry as this will help to focus your mind when choosing what to take, and what to leave behind.

It goes without saying that the lighter your rucksack, the more pleasant your trip will be. If taking a stove then simple ways to reduce weight include taking only one pan. This obviously requires a meal that can be prepared with one pan, which may be best practised at home first. Boil-in-the-bag meals may be heavier than dried food but have the advantage of not requiring any washing up to be done. If boiling food like pasta then use the water to make a packet soup. This will help to rehydrate you and provide a welcome hot drink. Cook outside your tent or in the porch to minimise condensation and reduce the risk of burning the tent down!

Look to minimise weight with your choice of each item of equipment and consider clothing that fulfils more than one function. Be ruthless with your packing and on returning from your trip review what you took. Being honest about whether you really needed it all will help the next time you pack. Some packing decisions come down to comfort, like whether to take a very thin lightweight sleeping mat, or something thicker and more comfortable. In the end, it's all about compromise!

Choose a tent which is light, strong and easy to put up. Look for a hard-wearing groundsheet, good ventilation, strong zips and good quality poles. As mentioned in Chapter 3, the winds are much stronger in the hills than in the valleys, and a tent designed for valley camping may be unsuitable for the uplands - it may get destroyed (quite literally) by strong winds. In the height of summer with a very good forecast then a less robust tent may work fine. But as with all aspects of hill walking, get a forecast, plan a route and assess if you and your kit are up to the challenge.

CAMPING AND THE ENVIRONMENT

Ensuring that wild camping does not adversely affect the upland environment can be achieved by following some straightforward guidelines. Simply put, with no facilities at hand you need to think carefully about your impact – both physical and visual. Here are some suggestions:

- Whenever you wild camp leave the site as you find it.

- Keep your group small and as discreet as possible.

- Camp away from popular areas – your presence may attract other campers to your unofficial 'site'.

- Be inconspicuous. A green tent may blend into the landscape whereas a brightly coloured tent can spoil the view. It is best to remove your tent during the day, especially where other walkers are likely to pass by.

- Camp in one place for only 1 or 2 nights and on dry / well-drained ground that won't be easily damaged.

- Pitch the tent in a way that avoids having to cut drainage ditches or move boulders. If you do have to move large stones replace them later.

- Try to avoid picking a site that means you have to cross sensitive areas to collect water or go to the toilet.

- If the campsite is on soft or boggy ground pitch the tents further away from each other, this will minimise trampling between tents.

- Litter – plan ahead. If you brought it all in you should be able to take it all out! Carry out all litter – even biodegradable material is slow to

STAYING OUT IN WINTER

Camping in winter

decompose in the mountain environment and may be scattered by animals. Do not dig rubbish in to the ground or try to hide it under boulders. Try to take away any other litter left by people less considerate than you.

- Fires can be highly destructive. Apart from the risks to you, wild fires can be very damaging to vegetation. Heathland fires on blanket bog can burn into the peat and destroy the habitat. The limited amounts of dead wood in the uplands are also essential habitats for the insects on which birds and other animals feed. Charred fire sites are also unattractive. Use a stove for cooking, and to keep warm put on more clothes or get in your sleeping bag.

- Clean, pure water is a valuable resource relied upon by many people living in upland areas. The nutrient content of streams is generally low, and altering this by adding pollutants and soap could kill local insect and plant life. If you have to wash, dispose of soapy water well away from water courses. All toilet areas must be at least 30 metres from water (see Chapter 7 – Sanitation). Always consider your impact downstream.

Camping in winter is obviously more demanding than in summer for a variety of reasons. Here are some things to consider:

- Site choice can be more important in winter. The ground may be frozen in the evening, but a rapid overnight thaw may reveal that you pitched a tent on a now not-so-frozen bog!

- Pegs are unlikely to be reliable anchors in snow. Use boulders, ice axes and buried bags of snow.

- Ground insulation is crucial to a good night's sleep. Take a good foam or self-inflating mattress.

- When cooking avoid having to melt snow as it is slow and uses a lot of fuel. Find running water if you can.

- If possible keep the tent ventilated at night to reduce condensation.

Carry out all litter

Leave no trace after snow holing

Snow shelters

If planning to stay out for a night in the hills a snow shelter can provide a more secure alternative to camping. There are a variety of issues to consider, such as site choice, none of which are covered here. Instead, a summary of emergency snow shelters is provided.

The ability to improvise shelter can be a life saver if it is not possible to walk out. In essence, this involves digging into compact snow to escape from the wind and create a pocket of still air. Different snow conditions dictate that different types of shelter are constructed, but typically, a snow hole is dug into a bank of firm snow.

A small hole can be dug out with an ice axe in an emergency but if planning to spend a night out, take a snow shovel to dig a proper snow hole. The overriding reason for digging an emergency snow hole is to seek shelter from the elements.

When deciding on a location for a snow hole or emergency shelter be aware of possible changing conditions - might the wind direction change and plug up the entrance to the hole, with the potential to suffocate you? Is a thaw forecast, which could result in the snow above collapsing upon you?

This is but the briefest of summaries of snow shelters. Comprehensive advice is available in *Winter Skills* published by Mountain Leader Training.

Cut hole snug so minimal heat is lost to the air

Push ice axe through wall for ventilation

Backward slope to seat prevents 'drifting' forward if sleep occurs

Use everything in pack for insulation: sit on pack etc.

Downward slope to entrance allows cold air to leave

Partially block the entrance with snow

An emergency snow shelter

CHAPTER 7

SANITATION

There's a reluctance to talk about what is one of our most natural functions! And yet by not thinking carefully about this we can endanger human health and potentially poison the upland environment.

©Simon Norris

Drinking from a mountain stream

Lightweight collapsible camping trowel **Inset:** *Closed trowel*

PROTECT FRESH WATER

A mountain stream is often seen as the epitome of purity – so don't pollute it. Streams are a vital source of fresh water for hill farmers and for campers. It will also be a home to, or a water source for, wildlife.

• Ensure you are at least 30 metres away from running water when you defecate.

• When camping, defecate and urinate downhill from your campsite; collect drinking water from above your camp.

LEAVE NO TRACE

It can be an unpleasant and unnecessary souvenir to encounter human waste on a path or close to a crag.

• Be considerate of others and defecate at least 50 metres from paths and 200 metres from huts and crags.

• Carry a lightweight trowel and when digging carefully cut out and replace the top turf.

• Dig a hole 15 cm (6") deep to bury your excrement. If this is not possible, keep well away from paths and spread the excrement thinly to increase the rate of its decomposition (squashing it under a boulder will slow decomposition). On especially sensitive high plateaux, excrement should be carried down to less sensitive locations for burial, or even better, carried out.

• The smell from urine and excrement is unpleasant. Avoid doing either in enclosed spaces (caves, ruined buildings etc), at the foot of crags or behind huts.

• Consider using a 'pee bottle'.

• In snow, dig down into the soil. Give a thought to the consequences when the snow melts!

'Accessories'

Toilet paper and female sanitary towels are slow to decompose and may be dug up by animals.

• Carry it out if possible. Come prepared with plastic bags – dog poo bags are ideal for the purpose. Tampons and sanitary towels should be carried out – plastic screw-top containers are convenient.

CHAPTER 8

ACCESS AND THE ENVIRONMENT

Mountain landscapes may seem vast and our presence in them inconsequential. However, all land belongs to someone so we must act in a considerate and responsible manner, to preserve access and conserve the environment.

ACCESS LEGISLATION

The Countryside Rights of Way Act 2000 (CRoW) is the main piece of legislation governing access to the uplands of England and Wales. The CRoW Act defined areas of mountain, moor, heath, down and registered common land as open access land. If you are unsure of your rights and responsibilities, or where you can go, then visit **www.countrysideaccess.gov.uk**

Public rights of way

The Public Rights of Way (PRoW) network in England and Wales is a unique asset. Rights of way are minor public highways, and it is important to understand what types of PRoW may be used for different activities. They include: footpaths (where the right of way is on foot only); bridleways (for pedestrians, horse riders and cyclists); restricted byways (open to all traffic except motorised vehicles); and byways open to all traffic (BOATS).

The restrictions that are sometimes used on CRoW access land do not affect public rights of way (so you can walk along them even when surrounding access land is closed). However, public rights of way can sometimes be diverted, removed, created or have the rights suspended but only by the local highway authority. Official signs, posted by the authority, will be found on the route to tell you if there are any changes to the local network.

Permissive access

The BMC liaises with landowners and conservation bodies where necessary to negotiate voluntary access arrangements. The BMC also has a network of over 30 local access representatives to ensure any access or conservation issues are resolved.

Access in England & Wales in principle...

Access is all about balancing the 'Three Rs' – rights, responsibilities and restrictions. Where we enjoy a right of access, this must be used responsibly. On occasion, restrictions based on a least restrictive approach may be needed to protect conservation interests. The BMC works to ensure successful access management, where all parties recognise and respect the legitimate interests of others and where recreation and conservation benefit mutually.

... and in practice

Restrictions on access are often agreed to protect important species of plants or animals and must be observed. If you have any doubts about these, abide by them while you are in the hills and then contact the BMC to discuss the reasons for them.

Hill walking across open access land

In some situations access is only secured by years of sensitive negotiation with landowners and conservation bodies. The BMC always ensures that the least restrictive option is achieved. Ignoring restrictions could aggravate a delicate situation and at worst lead to the withdrawal of access.

Access in Scotland

Different access legislation and guidelines apply to Scotland, where there is a freedom of access across almost all land. These rights were made statutory through the Land Reform (Scotland) Act 2003. For guidance see the *Scottish Outdoor Access Code* at **www.outdooraccess-scotland.com**

Gates and fences

These are usually erected to control the movement of stock and prevent overgrazing of sensitive areas, not to keep people out. Please leave gates as you find them and avoid damage to walls and fences by using the gates and stiles provided.

Dogs

It is a criminal offence to allow your dog to worry stock. On open access land in England and Wales dogs must be kept on a short lead from 1st March to 31st July and at all times when in the vicinity of livestock. They may be excluded at all times on some grouse moors. In fields of adult animals they must be kept under close control on a short lead. Landowners are legally empowered to shoot any dog that is causing distress to grazing animals if they believe this is the only way to stop it. Dogs can cause other problems – disturbing wildlife, barking, disrupting other users, defecating near paths or along the bottom of cliffs. Always consider the interests of others who use the land – not everyone will love your dog as much as you do.

Leave gates as you find them

To protect moorland birds

DOGS ARE NOT PERMITTED ON THIS ACCESS LAND

(COUNTRYSIDE & RIGHTS OF WAY ACT 2000, SECTION 23 RESTRICTION)

This does not apply to dogs on public rights of way, guide dogs, hearing dogs, or dogs for which the owner or occupier of this land has given consent.

THE UPLAND ENVIRONMENT

We can all minimise our impact by planning ahead and preparing before going out onto the hills. The weather, the relative fragility of the location and its popularity can all affect our impact.

Much can be done to minimise erosion and disturbance by applying common sense:

- Scree slopes provide an important ecological habitat but can easily be eroded – so keep off them unless there is absolutely no other route.

- Try walking within an erosion scar rather than around it, thereby reducing the risk of enlarging the eroded area, or avoid eroded areas completely if there is an alternative.

- Think about your route. For example, repeated kicking of steps causes much of the initial damage on steep slopes; avoid this by zig-zagging across such slopes.

- Noise by groups or individuals can affect the hill walking experience for others – be considerate.

Use existing paths to minimise upland erosion

Wild fires

Both peat and vegetation which grow in many of our upland areas can become dry and flammable, particularly during the summer. Accidental fires can destroy natural habitats and can kill animals and birds. Do not light fires on moorlands – not even gas stoves or barbecues and never stub matches or cigarettes out in the vegetation. Respect all warning signs and if you see a fire, don't assume that someone else has called the emergency services. Note your location and dial 999.

Paths

Paths have been constructed in many areas to protect and repair mountains from the erosion that is caused by the sheer volume of visitors. Use these paths wherever possible rather than taking shortcuts. Similarly, drainage channels and culverts are essential to take surface water away from paths and should not be blocked or dammed in any way. Paths are often only the width of one person; walkers should walk in single file on such sections.

Cairns and memorials

The BMC does not support the use of waymarks, cairns or other intrusive features, other than those traditionally established on summits and path junctions. Some cairns are important landmarks but most are an unnecessary intrusion and detract from the character of a wild and remote setting.

Building cairns exacerbates erosion and is the mountain equivalent of graffiti, so don't do it. While we sympathise with the grief that the bereaved feel, memorial artefacts should not be a feature of the mountain landscape and nothing should be done without formal landowner consultation and agreement.

Boundaries

Boundaries such as dry stone walls are traditional structures that can be historical features in themselves and important aspects of the landscape. Climbing over boundary walls and fences will damage them; walls are very expensive to repair and fences are often damaged when we step onto the galvanised wire. Use stiles and gates wherever possible and if you need to climb over, do so near to fence posts or where the wall appears strongest.

Litter

None of us like seeing discarded wrappers and plastic bottles in the mountains. Both wild and domestic animals may injure themselves on discarded litter. Landowners can also restrict access onto private land as a result of littering.

- Take your litter home with you – if you've carried it in, you can carry it out.

- Where it is safe and not too unpleasant, pick up other people's litter (especially non-biodegradable material).

- Organic litter such as fruit peel takes longer to break down than most people think. It also attracts certain predator species, so take it home.

- Reduce the litter you need to carry out with you by repackaging your food before you set out.

Using public transport eases traffic congestion in the uplands

Transport

Traffic congestion and parking problems are an issue in many popular upland areas, particularly during popular times. You can make a difference by taking public transport, car sharing and using designated parking places. Money from car parks can be used for environmental work in the local area, so consider parking charges in that context.

Shop locally

The local spending of climbers, hill walkers and mountaineers is vital to the conservation and development of many mountain regions. Wherever possible, shop and buy locally from independent stores (e.g. groceries, technical equipment, local cafes and restaurants).

CHAPTER 9

EMERGENCY PROCEDURES
AND FIRST AID

Mountain incidents range from inconvenient to
life threatening. There is no golden rule on how
to act but there are some well established principles.

What to do

In the event of an incident in the hills, stay calm, and take time to assess the situation before deciding what to do. Consider what should be done immediately to safeguard you and the group you are with. If anyone is injured, remember ABC – airway, breathing, and circulation – which are explained in greater detail below. Treat any injuries, but remember the principle of "do no harm". Make any casualties warm and comfortable, placing any unconscious casualties in the recovery position.

Determine your exact position on the map and consider the options for:

• **Descent to safety** What will the terrain be like? How far to reach safety? Are you sure you can carry the casualty? Will the casualty's injuries be made worse by travelling?

• **Finding shelter** Don't use up valuable time and energy unless you are sure about finding shelter.

• **Staying put** Can your situation be resolved if you stay where you are?

• **Sending for help** Remember that even when a rescue team has been alerted help might not arrive for several hours.

SENDING FOR HELP

When an incident takes place in the hills, there are a number of services that can help. Collect your thoughts - the emergency services will need to know what has happened, the nature of the injuries and the position of the incident (including, if possible, the map grid reference). Mobile phone coverage is now good in most areas except in some of the deep valleys and, of course, underground. If no signal can be obtained, a reliable member of the party, with full information about the accident, should be sent to find the nearest telephone.

You need to consider whether you need an Ambulance or Mountain Rescue Team. If someone has fallen down a mine or into a natural cave, you are likely to need help from a Cave Rescue Team. If you are on a road, an ambulance is likely to be most appropriate. However, if the injured person is unable to walk or on dangerous terrain, a stretcher and a Mountain Rescue Team will be needed - dial the emergency number and ask for the Police, then Mountain Rescue. Confused? Don't worry, make the call to the emergency services, and they will pass your information on to the service best placed to respond.

Mountain Rescue Teams are equipped to a high standard and work closely with the Search and Rescue helicopters and Air Ambulance services. Consequently, only minor injuries should come within the scope of treatment and evacuation by the companions of the injured. The rule for all other cases is to make the casualty safe, to start first aid, and to send for the appropriate emergency service.

Try to remain calm and collected when phoning for help

When phoning for help

Dial 999 and ask for:
POLICE and then
MOUNTAIN RESCUE

When connected provide:

1. Location of the incident (grid reference, map sheet number, name of mountain area and description of the terrain).

2. Number and names of people in the party and their condition.

3. Any injuries and names of casualties.

Be ready to provide the following additional information:

- Telephone number of the phone you are using and any other phones in the group.

- The nature of the incident – what happened?

- Time of the incident.

- Weather conditions including wind speed and visibility at the accident site.

- Equipment which is at the accident site (warm clothing, group shelter etc.).

- Any distinguishing feature / marker / colour at the accident site.

- Location of where you are phoning from – if different from accident site.

If you have a mobile phone:

- Try to conserve battery life by having all the details to hand before phoning.

- If there is no mobile coverage at your location consider whether it might be worth moving to another location to phone from. Walking uphill is often the best way to find a better signal.

- Check who else in your party has a mobile phone (and coverage) and evaluate the amount of battery life available in the event of additional calls being necessary.

Lack of help

You have a difficult decision when the casualty is severely injured, possibly unconscious, and you are alone and unable to make a phone call. You should try to summon help from nearby climbers or walkers by shouting, giving the distress call on a whistle (6 blasts repeated regularly) or flashing a torch (6 flashes repeated regularly). If there is no response, assess the relative dangers of either leaving the casualty or failing to get help. Act decisively in the interest of the casualty, but not in ways that will endanger you.

A whistle is a great way to attract attention

If going for help on foot, remember to take all necessary information for when phoning for help. Write it down if possible.

- If possible, leave at least one person with the casualty.

- If possible, two or more people should go for help.

- Make the casualty's location easily seen by search parties.

What to do if a helicopter arrives

A helicopter may arrive before the Mountain Rescue Team. Extinguish all flames and secure all equipment. To attract the attention of the helicopter stand facing it with both arms up in the air making a Y shape. The downdraught can knock you over, so make sure you are in a safe position. Do not approach the helicopter until clearly signalled to do so by the pilot.

FIRST AID

Many people do not consider the importance of first aid training until standing next to an injured companion on a remote mountainside. However, a large range of first aid courses are available, many of which are tailored to hill walkers, climbers and mountaineers. A summary of some first aid treatment is given below, but it should not be seen as a substitute for professional first aid training.

General first aid treatment

While waiting for the emergency service, basic first aid treatment should be given. You should expect to feel apprehensive and worried, and on the edge of your 'comfort zone'. Having a system to work to helps you control your emotions and avoids you missing serious conditions. Think 'Safety, A, B, C, then D, E and F, if appropriate'. Is the casualty responsive? Talking to the casualty is the best way of getting information.

Safety – Are you and the casualty safe from further danger?
If not, try to make yourselves safe either by moving or anchoring yourselves.

A – Is the casualty's *airway* open?
If necessary, open the airway by lifting the chin and gently tilting the head backwards or, after trauma (physical injury), gently stabilise the neck in the straight-line (neutral) position with your hands and open the airway with a jaw thrust.

An open airway is essential; if the casualty is unconscious or semi-conscious, the tongue can fall back blocking the airway and cause death from asphyxia in minutes. After trauma, the neck may have been damaged. Try to avoid further movement of the neck **but** the priority is to ensure that the airway is open. As the jaw thrust is more difficult to perform, you may need to use the 'chin lift, head tilt' or even turn the casualty on to their side to drain vomit.

Continually check that the airway remains open, adjusting the casualty's position as required.

Take a first aid kit – and know how to use it!

B – Is the casualty *breathing*?

Look, feel and listen for breathing. Basic Life Support (cardiac compression and artificial respiration) should be started, if you are trained, when the casualty is unconscious and shows no signs of breathing, and it can be continued until help arrives, and where there is a chance of recovery (lightning, drowning, heart attack). It is usually futile in casualties with internal injuries and is probably best to defer in cases of severe hypothermia unless it develops instantly when you are there. An unconscious but breathing casualty should be put in the recovery position if possible. In cases involving trauma, take care that the neck remains supported and in a neutral position. Always check the airway is still open.

C – Is the *circulation* adequate?

Stop any bleeding from wounds by elevation and direct pressure with dressings or clothing. The pressure needs to be applied continuously for at least ten minutes. Internal bleeding should be suspected if the casualty has sustained blows to the chest or abdomen or broken thigh bone (femur). Loss of blood leads to shock; the casualty will look white, feel cold and be sweating. The pulse may be rapid and the casualty anxious. Lay the casualty down and possibly raise the legs. The condition often deteriorates and all steps should be taken to facilitate the rapid arrival of the Mountain Rescue Team and, if possible, a helicopter. A record of the pulse rate and conscious level is very helpful.

D – Is the casualty *disabled* due to damage to head or spine?

Record the casualty's conscious level – alert, responsive to voice, responsive to pain or unresponsive? Has the spine been damaged? If so, do not move the casualty unless essential for safety reasons. Maintain the head in the straight-line (neutral) position with your hands without pulling on the head.

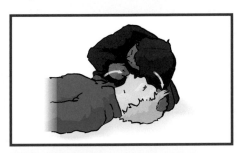

Lifting the chin and tilting the head back to open the airway. Looking, feeling and listening for signs of breathing

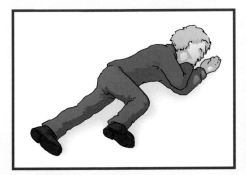

The recovery position

Maintaining the head in the straight-line (neutral) position

E – Prevent *exposure* (hypothermia)

Prevent exposure (hypothermia) by sheltering the casualty from the wind and rain. Wrap them in as many layers of clothing as possible and encased in a 'poly bag' or other impermeable barrier. Do not forget to insulate the head and underneath the casualty. Even mild hypothermia worsens the outcome of many injuries.

F – Check for *fractures*

If present, immobilise the limb by the simplest method available. In the case of the arm, pad it and bandage it to the chest, and in the case of the leg, pad it and bandage it to the other leg.

Hypothermia

This occurs when a person's heat loss exceeds their heat generation. To avoid hypothermia, use a two-pronged approach by dressing appropriately, and avoiding exhaustion. Modern mountain clothing is very effective at conserving heat in a wide range of climates. Wind resistance and keeping the surface of the body dry are important factors when choosing clothing. The best way of generating heat is muscular exercise. Bear in mind that to maintain this you should eat carbohydrate snacks and drink regularly during the day. Alcohol, even the previous night, can significantly reduce your endurance.

The symptoms of hypothermia start with feeling cold, apathy, clumsiness and stumbling followed by shivering. More severe hypothermia is recognised by confusion, lack of shivering, an inability to walk, and finally coma. In the early stages, increased insulation, warm drinks and carbohydrates should allow a retreat to safety by walking. Established, severe hypothermia is more difficult to manage as sudden movements of the casualty can precipitate a cardiac arrest. Insulate the casualty as best you can without disturbing their position too much and call for a Mountain Rescue Team. Even people with severe hypothermia showing no signs of life have been resuscitated successfully, but when to start Basic Life Support is complex and best discussed with the Mountain Rescue Team before you start.

For further hill and mountain specific information visit the Medical Advice section of the BMC website.

EMERGENCY BIVOUACS

An unintentional night out is not an uncommon incident, and can result from a navigational error or unexpected conditions. As such, it is one of those things a hill walker should be prepared for. As with many mountain incidents, such nights out can commonly be avoided with good planning, taking a headtorch and having an early start.

Appropriate clothing will conserve heat in even the worst conditions

Group shelters are perfect for emergency bivouacs

Emergency snow holes are covered at the end of Chapter 6, and as mentioned in Chapter 2, group shelters and bivi bags provide great protection from the elements.

If you are caught out, consider the following:

- Seek shelter from the elements.

- Put all your spare clothing on, including hats and gloves.

- Sit on anything that will provide insulation from the ground, such as your rucksack.

- Seek warmth from other party members by huddling together.

- Keep an eye on other people for signs of hypothermia.

Come first light, and if everyone is fine, continue with your journey. Get word out as soon as possible to put a stop to any potential search that has begun.

Further points to consider

Large, organised groups should bear in mind that the Mountain Rescue Teams are a finite resource and it is wrong to assume their availability. Prevention is better than First Aid! Most injuries are lower leg sprains and fractures, making the wearing of appropriate footwear essential. The majority of climbers killed in Britain as a result of a climbing accident die from a head injury. A helmet, whilst not being 100% effective, can make the difference between living and dying.

A GPS device, whilst being useful, is no substitute for carrying a map and compass, and knowing how to use them. The routine carrying of a suitable headtorch would save many needless call-outs. Whilst mobile phones can be very useful in emergencies, any temptation to use them in the hills to call the emergency services in non-emergency circumstances should be resisted. If you are not sure whether it is an emergency or not, please investigate a little yourself first before reaching for your phone.

Your mountain rescuers are unpaid volunteers and rely on charitable contributions. Your consideration and a 'Thank you' go a long way to ensure the service continues. Collection boxes are located in pubs and outdoor shops in most upland areas. You can also donate online at **www.mountain.rescue.org.uk/giving** and **www.mrcofs.org**

MOUNTAINEERING COUNCILS

British Mountaineering Council – BMC
177-179 Burton Road, Manchester M20 2BB
T 0161 445 6111   **E** office@thebmc.co.uk
www.thebmc.co.uk

Mountaineering Council of Scotland – MCofS
The Old Granary, West Mill Street, Perth PH1 5QP
T 01738 638227   **E** info@mcofs.org.uk
www.mcofs.org.uk

Mountaineering Ireland – MI
Sport HQ, 13 Joyce Way, Park West Business Park,
Dublin 12, Ireland
T 00 353 (1) 625 1115 **E** info@mountaineering.ie
www.mountaineering.ie

MOUNTAIN LEADER TRAINING BOARDS

Mountain Leader Training
MLT, Siabod Cottage, Capel Curig, Conwy LL24 0ES
T 01690 720272   **E** info@mltuk.org
www.mountainleadertraining.org

Mountain Leader Training England
MLTE, Siabod Cottage, Capel Curig, Conwy LL24 0ES
T 01690 720314   **E** info@mlte.org
www.mlte.org

Mountain Leader Training Wales
Hyfforddi Arweinwyr Mynydd Cymru
Siabod Cottage, Capel Curig, Conwy LL24 0ES
T 01690 720361   **E** info@mltw.org
www.mltw.org

Mountain Leader Training Scotland
Glenmore, Aviemore, Inverness-shire PH22 1QU
T 01479 861248   **E** smltb@aol.com
www.mountainleadertraining.org

Mountain Leader Training Northern Ireland
Tollymore, Bryansford, Newcastle, Co Down BT33 0PT
T 028 4372 2158   **E** admin@tollymore.com
www.mountainleadertraining.org

NATIONAL CENTRES

Plas y Brenin
Capel Curig, Conwy LL24 0ET
T 01690 720214   **E** info@pyb.co.uk
www.pyb.co.uk

Glenmore Lodge
Aviemore, Inverness-shire PH22 1BR
T 01479 861 256
E enquiries@glenmorelodge.org.uk
www.glenmorelodge.org.uk

Tollymore
Bryansford, Newcastle, Co. Down BT33 0PT
T 028 4372 2158   **E** admin@tollymore.com
www.tollymore.com

BOOKS

- Hill Walking *Steve Long, Mountain Leader Training, 2003*
  Mynydda *Steve Long, Mountain Leader Training, 2009*

- Navigation in the Mountains *Carlo Forte, Mountain Leader Training, 2011*

- Winter Skills *Andy Cunningham and Allen Fyffe, Mountain Leader Training, 2007*

- Crampons & Ice Axes *BMC, 2002*

- International Mountain Trekking *Plas y Brenin, Mountain Leader Training, 2011*

- The Green Guide to the Uplands *BMC, 2009*

- Young People: Climbing, Hill Walking, Mountaineering: A Parent's Guide *BMC, 2008*

- Walking for All: Disability Awareness in Hill Walking, *Michael Hunt, Mountain Leader Training England, 2011*

- Call Out Mountain Rescue: A Pocket Guide to Safety on the Hill *Mountain Rescue, 2008*

- Pocket First Aid and Wilderness Medicine *Drs Jim Duff and Peter Gormly, Cicerone, 2007*

- Weather for Hill Walkers and Climbers *Malcolm Thomas, Sutton Publishing, 1997*

- A Chance in a Million, Scottish Avalanches *Bob Barton & Blyth Wright, Scottish Mountaineering Trust, 2000*

DVDS

- Hill Walking Essentials *BMC, MCofS, MLTE, 2008*

- Winter Essentials *BMC, MCofS, MLTE, 2005*

- Alpine Essentials *BMC, MCofS, 2006*

- Off Piste Essentials *BMC, PyB, MCofS, 2008*

- Water Hazards in the Mountains *MCofS, 2002*

- Water Safety for Walkers *MCofS, 2002*

WEBSITES

- Mountain Weather Information Service
  www.mwis.org.uk

- The Met Office
  www.metoffice.gov.uk

- sportscotland Avalanche Information Service
  www.sais.gov.uk

- Mountain Rescue England & Wales
  www.mountain.rescue.org.uk

- Mountain Rescue Committee of Scotland
  www.mrcofs.org

- Mountain Bothies Association
  www.mountainbothies.org.uk

- Long Distance Walkers Association
  www.ldwa.org.uk

- Runsweet (advice for diabetics)
  www.runsweet.com

- Lyme Disease Action
  (information on tick borne diseases)
  www.lymediseaseaction.org.uk

ACKNOWLEDGEMENTS

Written by Jon Garside, BMC/MLTE Training Officer, with support from members of the BMC Training and Youth Committee. A number of people were very generous in contributing to this book: Dr John Ellerton wrote part of Chapter 9 and text written by Dr Cath Flitcroft was used in Chapters 6, 7 and 8. Thanks also to Adrian Japp, Mal Creasey and Tony Ryan for proof reading the text and providing useful feedback.

Photos and other images have been provided by Ben Winston (front cover), Alex Messenger, Allen Fyfffe, Jon Garside, Lyme Disease Action, Peak District National Park, Central Brecons Mountain Rescue Team, Trail magazine, Plas y Brenin, Lowe Alpine and Sea to Summit.

NOTES